American Business: The Last Hurrah?
Can we regain our competitive edge?

Terrance S. Hitchcock

American Business:
The Last Hurrah?

Can we regain our competitive edge?

Dow Jones-Irwin Homewood, Illinois 60430

This publication is designed to provide accurate and authoritative information in regard to the subject matter covered. It is sold with the understanding that the publisher is not engaged in rendering legal, accounting, or other professional service. If legal advice or other expert assistance is required, the services of a competent professional person should be sought.

From a Declaration of Principles jointly adopted by a Committee of the American Bar Association and a Committee of Publishers.

Library of Congress Catalog Card No. 81–68094

Printed in the United States of America

1 2 3 4 5 6 7 8 9 0 D 9 8 7 6 5 4 3 2

I dedicate this book to those I love . . . my family

Foreword

The contributors to this book have examined a series of complicated questions. All of these problems are linked, however, to the basic concern that inspired the author, Dr. Terrance S. Hitchcock, to initiate this personal project some six years ago. That concern is how the complex of private, for-profit organizations that collectively form the American business community can regain its position of leadership vis-á-vis competitors in other countries, while still discharging a host of major obligations to improve the quality of life in this country.

No single commentator could, of course, develop a comprehensive program for addressing all facets of this basic issue. Hence, the contributors were asked to focus on the aspect(s) of the issue that they, for reasons of expertise and interest, felt most willing to explore. Some selected one particular area, while others ranged across a variety of topics, all related to the fundamental issue.

Included among these topics were the following:

1. How American businesses can improve productivity.
2. How relations between management and workers (both organized and nonunion) can be strengthened.
3. How to insure that members of groups traditionally underrepresented in management positions have a chance to secure professional and management opportunities in business organizations and to compete effectively for top leadership roles.
4. How to promote government regulatory activities that will help achieve desirable social goals (e.g., clean air, pure water) while minimizing costs to business.
5. How to harness the energies and talents of the business community in solving pressing social problems, in addition to those that businessmen and women ordinarily encounter in the normal course of producing and delivering goods and services.

These topics, each of which represent a different aspect of the basic issue, are not, of course, mutually exclusive. Regulatory activities by government agencies, for example, are germane to many of the other facets of the basic issue (e.g., productivity or equal employment and advancement opportunities). Nevertheless, these specific topic areas, which continue to be the subject of searching debate in a variety of forums, did provide the contributors with some broad categories to which they could orient their observations and advice about the future of American business.

The range of views on the different topics indicates clearly that no "party line" was foisted on the contributors. Moreover, no single compendium of observations on the future of American business can exhaustively represent all the possible approaches to this issue. Dr. Hitchcock has assembled a diversity of opinions, which will alternatively challenge, confound, and reinforce the reader's own views and, it is hoped stimulate further analysis.

The impetus for this writing came from a series of discussions during 1974 and 1975 involving Dr. Hitchcock, then with the corporate human resource department of The Coca-Cola Company, and Gary Parker, a colleague of Dr. Hitchcock's at The Coca-Cola Company. As these conversations proceeded, the two became committed to the idea of conducting, on a personal basis, an extensive research project that would gather and assess the ideas of leading personalities in different spheres of American life about the challenges and opportunities that the 1980s would offer to this country's business community.

Aided by their research associate, Clifford Steele, Dr. Hitchcock and Mr. Parker embarked on an ambitious program of interviews, beginning in the middle 1970s. On occasion, the material gathered through the interviews was complemented by recent speech materials that the contributors felt were particularly relevant to the topics being explored.

I joined the project in late 1976 to assist Dr. Hitchcock in completing the interviewing and other research activities and in compiling a first draft of the manuscript. By this time Mr. Parker had been transferred out of the country and had had to discontinue his involvement.

Throughout 1977 and into the summer of 1978, Dr. Hitchcock and I worked, assisted by Clifford Steele, on the compilation of the original draft. Dr. Hitchcock and Mr. Steele then spent the last three years refining the draft manuscript, continuing to add new interviews and related materials as these were made available by the contributors.

Quite obviously, the development of this book has enjoyed the support and involvement of many people, including leaders in both the public and private sector, both in terms of the great variety of individuals who provided their insights and recommendations about the future of American business, and those who took part in editing and compiling the interview and research results into the final manuscript.

None of those who participated will pretend that the views expressed in this volume represent in any sense the final word of the different questions and problems that the contributors have addressed. All certainly share the hope that motivated Dr. Hitchcock to launch the project back in the mid-1970s, that a compendium of recommendations by informed observers about improving the performance of the U.S. business community in the 1980s would be useful to both business leaders and others whose decisions affect business prospects and conditions.

Similarly, serious dialogues on the topics discussed in the book did not begin with the initiation of Dr. Hitchcock's project. Indeed, it was the prospect of joining and strengthening the many discussions and analyses that were underway at the time the project was conceived that led Dr. Hitchcock and Mr. Parker to launch the effort in the first place. Hopefully, these dialogues will continue, with the contributions of those who participated in Dr. Hitchcock's project adding to our understanding about the future of American business in the current decade and beyond.

Dr. Clifford Hendrix

Preface

Historian Frederick Jackson Turner once said, "If mankind could once really understand what it has done and thought in the past, is it not possible that it would stumble along now and in the future with more intelligence and a more conscious purpose?"

In the spirit of Turner's statement, I saw the need, in 1976, to bring together business, labor, government, and education. The dream was to produce a combined effort to reflect on the past and present condition of American business and to consider the future directions that American business and our American society might take.

The result is this book, which stands as a forum in which national leaders from various circles of American life present their views and argue their points of view. The book is not meant to simply supply answers. It is a showcase for lively discussion and debate on some of the major topics concerning our business and economic life. It is meant to foster continued thinking and discussion and to focus what has often been to date confused arguments mired in ambiguous, undefined terms and uninformed positions. Most important, this volume is primarily meant to challenge the reader to question the current state of the American economy so that he or she may, in an informed manner, enter the debate and struggle, and take part in resolving the problems before us in the 1980s and 1990s.

We stand on the brink of the 21st century, already consumed in a world that is rapidly changing, year by year and even day by day. Alvin Toffler, in his landmark book *Future Shock,* characterized our society with such phrases as "the throw-away society," "the new nomads," "modular man," and "the fractured family." Toffler sketched a society in which swirling economic, political, and technological forces have begun to produce an environment devoid of direction and meaningful reference points. If we as a society are to make it successfully to the 21st century, we must redefine our direction and reference points, identify and address our problems, and search for definitions and solutions. Our problems are multiple and complex, products of more than 200 years of American history. Therefore answers will not appear overnight. The reader will quickly realize that the people contributing their thoughts to this book understand that America's business problems will take much time and effort to solve.

Most of the people included in this book were first interviewed in 1976 and 1977. In the few short years since, a great deal has happened in the world. Therefore each of the interviewees was contacted once again in January 1981 to reappraise his or her statements—to alter or update thoughts to fit current thinking. As a result, this book has a general tone. While at times addressing particular issues in detail, the discussion focuses on major problems and trends that have stood the test of time. They are matters that were with us in and before the 1970s. And they will obviously be with us in the coming decades. They are not merely lightning crises that will dim and lose their significance in a month or a year.

The primary contributors to this discussion of American business were:

I.W. Abel, Former President
United Steelworkers of America

William L. Batt, Former President
National Center for Productivity and
Quality of Working Life

W.T. Beebe, Chairman of the Board
Delta Air Lines

Caroline Bird, Author and Lecturer
"The Two Paycheck Marriage," "Born Female,"
"The Invisible Scar," "The Case Against College"

Julian Bond, State Senator
State of Georgia

Frank Borman, President and Chief Executive Officer
Eastern Air Lines

Thornton Bradshaw, Chairman of the Board and
Chief Executive Officer
RCA

D.W. Brooks, Chairman of the Board
Gold Kist, Inc.

Edmund G. ("Jerry") Brown, Jr., Governor
State of California

Ramsey Clark
Former Attorney General of the United States

John K. Collings, Jr., Vice Chairman
The Coca-Cola Company

Malcolm L. Denise, retired Vice President,
Labor Relations
Ford Motor Company

Henry Duncombe, Former Vice President
and Chief Economist
General Motors Corporation

Edward J. Feeney, President
Edward J. Feeney Associates

Fred K. Foulkes, Professor
Boston University

Wyche Fowler, Jr., U.S. Representative
State of Georgia

Chester Gadzinski, Former President and
Chief Executive Officer
Kearney National

Walter B. Gerken, Chairman of the Board and
Chief Executive Officer
Pacific Mutual

C. Jackson Grayson, Jr., President
American Productivity Center

Peter E. Haas, President
Levi Strauss & Co.

Anne Harlan, Project Director
Wellesley College Center for Research on Women

James L. Hayes, President
American Management Associations

Blackburn H. Hazlehurst, Former Chairman
of the Board
Hazlehurst & Associates

Donald P. Jacobs, Dean, J.L. Kellogg
Graduate School of Management
Northwestern University

David N. Judelson, President
Gulf & Western Industries

Herman Kahn, Chairman
Hudson Institute

Donald M. Kendall, Chairman and
Chief Executive Officer
PepsiCo, Inc.

Juanita M. Kreps
Former Secretary of Commerce of the United States

Felix E. Larkin, Chairman
W.R. Grace & Co.

Sally Levy, Director of Sales & Custom Conventions
Orleans Transportation Service

George Cabot Lodge, Professor
Harvard University

Thomas R. Masterson, Professor
Emory University

Paul W. McCracken, Professor
University of Michigan

Richard B. Norment IV, Managing Director
of Public Affairs
National Association of Manufacturers

Thomas H. Paine, Partner
Hewitt Associates

Frances Knight Palmeri, Editor and Publisher
Women's Work

Milton L. Rock, Senior Partner
Hay Associates

Dean Rusk
Former Secretary of State of the United States

Keizo Saji, Chairman and President
Suntory Limited

Karl P. Sauvant
Centre of Transnational Corporations, United Nations

George Sherman, President
George Sherman Associates

Robert E. Sibson, President
Sibson & Company

Grant G. Simmons, Jr., Former Chairman of the Board
Simmons Corporation

Jack D. Steele, Dean
University of Southern California

Arthur R. Taylor, Managing Partner
Arthur Taylor & Co.

Arthur B. Toan, Jr., Retired Partner
Price Waterhouse & Co.

R.E. "Ted" Turner, President
Turner Broadcasting System, Inc.

John R. Van de Water, President
John R. Van de Water Associates

Rawleigh Warner, Jr., Chairman of the Board
Mobil Oil Corporation

J.S. Webb, Vice-Chairman of the Board
TRW, Inc.

William Winpisinger, President
International Association of Machinists

Andrew Young
Former United States Representative
to the United Nations

In addition to these 51 men and women, the views of several important figures, including former President Gerald Ford, former Secretary of State Henry Kissinger, former Cabinet officer Elliott Richardson, and various members of Congress, are quoted at length. And beyond that, there are literally hundreds of other people who have expressed their views and given advice, helping me greatly in shaping this book. I would like to thank all of them, but in particular I must thank, Dr. Clifford Hendrix, Clifford A. Steele, Judy M. Miller, the Reverend Donald Clapp, Gary L. Parker, and James Toedtman.

Terrance S. Hitchcock

Acknowledgments

To the following individuals whose direct or indirect interest and support helped make this book reality:

A. B. Padgett, Dan Sweat, Leo Conroy, Andrew Felton Brimmer, I. W. Carmack, Gene E. Dyson, Henry J. Egen, Ernest Lotito, Joan Pinck, Ernest J. E. Griffes, Eli Ginzberg, Robert L. Berra, Henry F. Kelleher, Michael W. Moynihan, Chris Christopher, Warren Bennis, Governor George Busbee, Neil C. Churchill, Peter F. Drucker, John L. Holcomb, Clarence M. Kelly, Lester Maddox, David Mathews, Allen W. Mathis, Jr., Margaret Mead, Hollis Moore, Betty Southard Murphy, Governor William W. Scranton, Roger Wilkins, Willard Wirtz, Warren J. Wittreich, Thomas E. Wood, J. B. Fuqua, Jerome E. Vielehr, Gibson Winter, Elizabeth Finley, Paul Tillich, Sharon Myers, James Clayman, Sam Large, Beverly Kievman, Nancy Murry, Elmer Messerschmidt, Archie Rankin, Walter Krupp, James A. Russo, Carmen Norwine, Matt J. Murphy, Marshall Seybold, J. Paul Austin, Mercy Azar, Allison Geballe, Pete Moffett, Alex Haley, W. H. Ross, Carlton Curtis, Burton E. Bauder, Albert Swett, Michael W. D. McMullen, Father John Mulroy, Elizabeth Jagger, Gloria Lemos, Griffin Bell, William L. Cambre, George DeMore, S. I. Hawakawa, David Hughes III, Richard J. Smith, William M. Kelly, Jr., Kay Wagner, Roy Wennerholm, Beverly Freeman, Pam Leftwich, David Hamelin, Richard Adamkiewicz, Austin Kronemeyer, Daniel Bell, Richard Kendro, James D. Brown, Jere Smith, Claire Buckelew, Lucretia Coleman, Robert Burgin, Joel Martinez, William McGrath, Robert Dannemann, Walter Gansser, Nick Natiello, Robert T. Johnson, Edward Sewell, William Steele, Julian Goodman, Joseph Brennan, Robert Lester, James Bowers, Roger Nunley, Carl Menk, Douglas M. Adams, Patrick J. Alcox, Gerald McDonough, Bridge Hunt, Austin Kiplinger, Edward M. Kennedy, Vito Kuraitis, William Mahr, James V. O'Brien, Merrill Ruge, Remy Schaul, Fred Ulrich, Charles Turner, and Richard Yutendale.

Contents

1

Regulations

Few questions fuel the passions as the subject of regulation does among observers and analysts of the American business scene. In part, these strong feelings can be traced to ideology. For those who view themselves as embattled defenders of unfettered free enterprise, government regulation epitomizes many of the evils attendant upon government's interventions into economic affairs. Even advocates of such interventions feel that regulation has become oppressive and merits at least some measure of criticism.

Today government regulation is accelerating at an alarming rate. The cries from business become louder each day that it must be held in check. In one sense, the type of government control is as old as the Sherman Antitrust Act, updated and extended by the creation of the Federal Trade Commission. In another sense, it breaks entirely new ground. For example, consider the concerted effort and antitrust activity against IBM and AT&T and attempts at breaking up companies in

1

such so-called concentrated industries as steel, automobiles, oil, etc. Donald M. Kendell, chairman and chief executive officer of PepsiCo, Inc., suggests that "government regulation will always be with us. But there is no sense in letting the present trend continue, allowing government to get out of hand, when, by waking up to the situation and putting forth the required effort, we can live with regulation and hold it in check."[1]

Not surprisingly, self-interest also has a great deal to do with the intensity of views expressed on the issue of regulation. Georgia state senator Julian Bond has spoken directly to this point.

"I remember President Ford announcing that he was interested in some deregulation in the trucking industry. Here you see the giants saying, 'No, we want to be regulated and we don't want a completely free-market system,' while the smaller real independent entrepreneur was saying, 'Yes, we do want deregulation. We do want the freedom to let rates fall where they may.'"[2]

Aggravating these aspects of the debate is the absence of any systematic definition or any comprehensive framework in which a discussion of the regulation issue can proceed. Surely such a lack of definition is not unique to this particular question. Many issues that enjoy widespread public comment suffer from similar limitations. Nevertheless, as I hope this chapter will establish, the lack of precision about the elements of the regulation issue and about possible solutions to the problem is a defect that requires immediate attention. Greater precision is not only within our reach. It would also allow us to use the energy now consumed by passionate, partisan, and often useless arguing for more productive analysis.

The trouble with regulation

The interview participants meant many things when they referred to *government regulation*. To some, the term refers primarily to the decisions

and policies of the various bureaucratic components of the federal executive establishment. It includes the elements of the Cabinet Departments
(e.g., the Occupational Safety and Health Administration in the Department of Labor—OSHA
is a favorite whipping boy), the "independent"
regulatory agencies (e.g., the Interstate Commerce
Commission, the Federal Trade Commission, the
Civil Aeronautics Board), and the other agencies
that fit into neither of the previous categories (e.g.,
the Federal Energy Administration, the Energy
Research and Development Administration). Of-
fensive policies included, but were not limited to,
burdensome and/or duplicative reporting requirements, imposition of environmental standards,
and meddling with management prerogatives.

To Herman Kahn, chairman of the Hudson Institute, "Regulations were inadequate in many
areas, but it did not mean that we needed more,
only better quality."

Dr. John Van de Water, as president of Van de
Water Associates, consultants to management,
discussed freedom of choice.

"In private enterprise, the free market should
have considerable freedom, under the law, to influence proper compensation, without allowing
arbitrary discrimination. Yet, the unanimous recommendations for aiding the advance of the
economies in the underdeveloped and developing
nations, as stated in the Brandt Commission Report, *North-South* (M.I.T. Press), should be given
the most serious consideration. In the public sector, strikes, arbitration, fact-finding recommendations, or other means should not replace publicly
elected trustees and their responsibility for making final decisions on the payment of publicly employed non supervisory and managerial employees,
subject to determined standards of equivalency
with the private sector; yet public management
and public trustees need professional assistance
and knowledge to accomplish their role properly.

"Where are we headed? I believe, as Senator
Barry Goldwater (R–Ariz.) so well expresses it in

his 1976 book, *Coming Breakpoint*, that a free economy may not endure where government costs, at taxpayer expense, continue to grow at an alarming rate. As President Ford once stated, more than 100,000 federal employees spend their time simply writing and interpreting regulations. The burden upon private enterprise that results from this is staggering. As former Secretary of Labor John Dunlop suggested, our taxpayer-government costs of trying to help the underprivileged are reaching proportions where the effect on the economy can only hurt the underprivileged, as well as everyone else. It has been suggested that it will not be long before the average American must spend all of his working hours from January 1 to the end of June to pay his taxes. We must get across the fact that, as so often stated, there are no free lunches".

Grant Simmons, former chairman of Simmons Corporation (a multimillion-dollar manufacturer of bedding furniture, fabrics, and lamps), spoke strongly on regulation.

"The American public is already paying a tremendous price for the government's interference in business. For example, at enormous expense, the government is trying to break up an institution called IBM, one of the most skillfully and beautifully organized human institutions ever. There isn't anything about that company that isn't sparkling clean and very carefully thought out. It has the most beautiful track record you can possibly imagine, and it is a national asset of enormous value. By breaking up IBM, the government and the public are kicking themselves right where it hurts most. The government is a terrible bull in a china shop, and too often abuses its sovereign power by running in all directions."

Col. Frank Borman, chairman of Eastern Airlines, questions regulations as he defined the free enterprise system.

"The idea of a free enterprise system under government regulation may seem to be unique or completely paradoxical. In other words, how can you have a free enterprise system operating under stringent government regulations? Can you? Should it be changed? It is an appropriate discussion and a spirited debate in society today. Before anyone can make a case, in my estimation, for government regulation, you have to decide that the service that is to be regulated is essential to the society as a whole and that it serves its purpose best—serves society best—with some form of regulation."

To others, the complaint is primarily against Congress, particularly its passage of legislation, which fosters objectionable policies that promote and aggravate the bureaucratic activities just referred to by Borman. If the criticisms can be summarized, however, they are that these various forms of regulation cost too much, that they exact too heavy a toll in terms of the personal freedom of those involved in American business life, and that regulatory activities give excessive power to unelected bureaucrats.

Although these concerns are quite comprehensive in their scope, the interviewees were not equating regulation with all forms of government intervention in the economy. Macroeconomic considerations, such as deficit spending, tax policies, and Federal Reserve activities regarding interest rates, were outside the scope of the comments on regulation. Instead, comments focused primarily on those government activities that, in various ways, impeded the effective management of individual businesses.

Arguments against regulation on financial grounds were advanced by a number of the respondents. W. T. ("Tom") Beebe, chairman of the board of Delta Air Lines, was particularly concerned about the effects of regulation on small business. "Government has to quit harassing business, especially small business, with multitudes of agencies, all coming one after another, bringing up many of the same topics over and over again, but to different groups."

Similarly, Donald Kendall, chairman of PepsiCo

and current chairman of the U. S. Chamber of Commerce, described the financial burdens that business has to bear in complying with various reporting requirements. He cited the Quarterly Report of Wages form as one example of the costly forms business is forced to complete and submit. According to Kendall, this form alone costs the public $200 million annually. The government spends $30 million each year just to process the Quarterly Reports once they are submitted. The Quarterly Report is by no means the sole offender, according to Kendall. "To measure and find ways to reduce the costs of paperwork alone, the government has set up its own Commission on Federal Paperwork. It estimates that the various federal agencies are now producing, each year, 10 billion sheets of forms, applications, and reports, at an annual cost to taxpayers of $40 billion."

The additional costs to society that these regulations impose were also noted by Dr. Henry Duncombe, former chief economist for General Motors. Duncombe reported that the emission controls required of automobile manufacturers in the United States are adding steadily to the cost of each new car. By the middle of the 1980s, he projects that these costs will run over $1,000 per unit. Duncombe did not project the costs to society of *not* including these control devices—for example, the impact of increased pollution on health and the environment. He did, however, raise very basic questions about the overall implications of the government's pollution control program. "There are two questions that the economists raise: Will the consumer or society get benefits commensurate with the expenditure? And what is the cost effectiveness; that is, given a society's desire to spend that much money, is that the best way to do it?"

According to one report, putting into effect nationwide the Occupational Health and Safety Administration's standard of a 90-decibel maximum in the workplace will cost in the neighborhood of $13 billion. If the more stringent standards recommended by the Environmental

Protection Agency (EPA) are adopted, the costs of implementing the required changes would exceed $30 billion.

In summarizing his critique of government regulation in its various forms, Donald Kendall estimates that all such regulation costs the average American family $2,000 a year. Whether or not this estimate is precisely accurate, it is clear that there are substantial costs associated with the different forms of regulation. The key issue voiced by Henry Duncombe (i.e., whether the costs are justified) was not directly answered in the comments of the respondents. However, most would probably, as a group, identify readily with the sentiments of Paul McCracken, chairman of the Council of Economic Advisors under President Nixon.

"On balance, there is far too much government regulation, and the evidence is accumulating rapidly about the deleterious effects on the material welfare of people. The major beneficiaries of this overregulation are members of the bureaucracy who administer it and the interest groups who crouch behind these artificial shelters."

The development of an answer to Duncombe's question will be a major challenge for business in the coming years.

Will 1984 come in the 1980s?

The second line of criticism lodged against the current forms of government regulation emphasizes the political and civil liberties consequences; economics is secondary. George Sherman president of George Sherman Associates (a management consulting firm specializing in productivity and incentive systems) refers to "Big Brotherism" in his critique of the current system of regulation.

"Right now, we are at a high tide of Big Brotherism. Big Brother knows better than you do what is good for you. He wants to make you take the keys out of your car and dictate to you to stop smoking. He is going to propagandize and lecture to you, at the very least. He covers the whole government spectrum, getting involved in every facet of our lives."

In the political realm, a number of questions have been raised about the scope and extent of the regulations issued by the federal bureaucracy pursuant to the administration of statutes passed by Congress. Representative Elliott Levitas (D-Ga.) feels that the regulations promulgated by the bureaucracy usurp power. (Here *bureaucracy* primarily refers to the Cabinet Departments and the independent organizations, rather than to the so-called regulatory agencies.)

"Congressional veto of administrative rules and regulations addresses a most serious question: Who makes the laws in this country? Is it the elected Congress or the unelected bureaucrats who rule by administrative fiat?

"Time and time again the administrative agencies have usurped the authority of Congress through their quasi-legislative process of rule making. We have seen our legislative efforts frustrated or distorted when the implementing rules and regulations are published. The administrative agencies have often promulgated rules that are oppressive, arbitrary, or go clearly beyond the intent of Congress in passing the enabling act. Once the pithy little clause 'The Secretary shall have the power to promulgate regulations' is inserted in an act, it is your guess and mine how far the administrative agency will go or how lenient it will be.

"Americans are becoming increasingly cynical, frustrated, and angry with their government. If we look just at the sheer number of regulations promulgated within a year, we can understand the extent of their anger. In 1974, the bureaucracy adopted 7,496 new or amended regulations. During that same period, Congress passed 404 laws—a ratio of more than 18 to 1. It becomes clear who is running the lives and businesses of the citizens of this country—unelected bureaucrats, not elected representatives.

"The means of recourse presently available to our citizens are limited. Judicial review is a costly process prohibitive to the average citizen when a decision may be put off for years and particularly when the scope of judicial review is circumscribed. This government belongs to the people of this country. It should not oppress them. It should serve them. It should be responsive to them. In recent years, the government has not always acted in this fashion."[3]

Congressional concern over the whole matter of bureaucratic issuance of regulation is not limited to Representative Levitas. Legislation that he proposed to address this concern enjoyed the co-sponsorship of 156 of Levitas' House colleagues.

Interpretations of the current system

Regulation in its social context

It would not be accurate to suggest that any of the respondents were forceful apologists for the methods and procedures associated with current regulatory activities. Nevertheless, a number of the respondents did at least attempt to explain (if not to justify) the elements of the present system in terms of recent economic and social developments. Among those adopting such a posture was R. E. ("Ted") Turner, chairman of the Turner Advertising Company and owner of the Atlanta Braves and the Atlanta Hawks, which are part of the Turner Broadcasting System. In his view, current regulatory efforts are a natural by-product of our complex modern society. Although he indicates a conviction that government regulation "has gone too far in too many areas," Turner nevertheless presents a rationale for increased regulation.

"As things become more complex you have to have directions. If our lives are going to continue to become more complex because of the technological revolution that is taking place, we will need additional regulations to go along with the changing circumstances."

Malcolm Denise, retired vice-president of labor relations for the Ford Motor Company, viewed the problems of regulation in a similar manner. Denise examined the phenomenon of increasing regulation not as a curse foisted upon the public, but at least in part as a reaction to social forces and social changes. His view attempts to break through the stereotypes of conniving, power-hungry politicians, harsh, unreasonable regulations, and a naive, unsuspecting citizenry.

"Where intervention now exists, vested interests in the status quo are established, and these interests will strongly resist change unless modified by some alternative form of intervention. Thus, proposals to decontrol oil or gas prices are accompanied by suggestions such as subsidies to consumers to ease the pain of change. Indeed, the notion of manipulating market forces directly through financial penalties and subsidies at the consumer level—as distinguished from the long-established practice of intervention through tax policies—seems to be an increasingly popular device in government circles.

"While a lot of this is 'political' in the invidious sense, it seems to me that there are pressures at work that make considerable government intervention into the workings of the marketplace not only inevitable, but necessary. The pressures stem from population growth, an increasingly complex and interdependent system, the knowledge explosion, the finite availability of many resources, and the huge research and development costs and capital requirements of some projects deemed socially desirable. They all create or reveal problems of pressing public concern that the free market is not equipped to handle.

"Over time the meaning of 'free enterprise' has changed. It used to be an ideological dogma to be passionately maintained in purity. It has become a system pragmatically judged to be the best to do many things—but not necessarily everything. I think the bright, younger, college-trained men and women who are taking over the management of business are quite comfortable with the concept of the 'mixed' or 'pluralistic' system that we have. The major debates really are over the specifics of what the mix should be.

"The basic thrust of our system is the concept of free enterprise, but it now could be more fairly described as one of limited free enterprise, if that is not a self-contradicting phrase. The limitations have increased quite rapidly in the past 10 or 15 years as the number and scope of areas subjected to government regulation or control have increased.

"Despite the current fashionability in political circles of talk about reducing regulation, the overall trend of intervention in the market is likely to continue upward, despite some changes in the mix. The public expects government to 'do something' about matters that annoy them, and this expectation has become too pervasive and ingrained to be changed very quickly. It's something like reducing government spending; everyone is for it in general, but nobody wants to affect adversely his own particular interests.

"We as a people tend to blame 'the politicians' for increasing government intrusion, accusing them as a group of insatiable appetites for power. While this unquestionably is a part of the picture, I think we the people have to shoulder a major part of the responsibility. So long as we—including professed free enterprisers—persist in blaming the politicians for our economic malaises, whether they are to blame or not, we will continue to send politicians to Washington who think they've been elected to 'do something.' If it takes further intervention to give the appearance of 'doing something,' that's what we'll get."

James L. Hayes, president of American Management Associations, supplements Malcolm Denise's thorough analysis by examining how individuals in business see regulation. He then expands his focus to study how the American public is a far more complex entity than one like-thinking body, which further debunks the simplistic fantasy that regulation merely browbeats a downtrodden people.

"Most people in business are hardworking and enjoy being good citizens. They react humanly to the subtle entrapment of some regulations, particularly when the regulator appears to be more interested in headlines than in conformity with the law. The proprietary nature of entrepreneurship, the secretive aspects of competition, the perception of responsibility for others' assets, and a healthy personal ambition combine into an attitude that leads businessmen and women to resist efforts to control their activities. To them, regulations are threats.

"All who are seriously concerned with the economic warp and woof of our society agree that business and government must serve the public interest. The public interest, however, is defined differently by consumer groups, unions, universities, and other groups. Each group is made up of diverse human beings, and every personality and taste is involved.

"Discussion—of regulation, deregulation, or any other subject—does work. It is democracy at work, and it works because it is us."

The observations offered by Richard B. Norment, managing director of public affairs for the National Association of Manufacturers, are relevant to the question of why the government undertakes regulatory activities to the degree it does presently. Norment observed that such activities have substantially increased in the past several decades and are, in part, the result of public pressures that come from disproportionately vocal fragments of the total public. And Norment, like Hayes, fully incorporates the idea of an extremely complex public into his conception.

"By and large, government's regulatory approach to business has been a reaction to what seems to be general public pressure. Each regulatory effort has its own constituency, consisting of issue activists, special interest groups, and portions of the general public that have an immediate interest in the subject area. In a true sense of responsibility to the principles of representative democracy, legislators and regulatory agencies respond to the pressures of these constituent "publics." There begins the problem. Unfortunately, all too often these subgroups and fragments of the total public interest are most visible to government because of efficient, vocal, and often highly visible lobbying. Thus they are perceived as being the will of the whole population or at least a majority. The result is that legislators and regulators work all to often with only limited information and lack an appreciation of the full consequences of their actions. When you combine this situation with the natural trait of government wanting to govern, the result is not only more involvement of government in business, but also an ineffective or counterproductive series of regulations."

Many of the respondents commented on the sheer scope and extent of the government's varied efforts at regulation. This scope help explain, in part, why many businessmen feel these efforts to be so burdensome. The greater stringency of the regulatory effort, as compared with earlier periods in this nation's history, is also relevant in this regard. Arthur B. Toan, Jr., former director of management advisory services for Price Waterhouse and Company, speaks to this point in some detail, placing the "blame" for the vast amount of regulation on one particular point in our history.

"Until fairly recently, most of the government regulatory standards were set at relatively low levels. Take laws affecting employee safety, for example. Most government regulations historically have dealt with keeping the worst offenders from being the worst offenders. One of the things that seems to have happened, starting in the 1960s, was that regulation shifted and went up much higher in the scale. Agencies set standards that were higher than even the best performers in the industry had achieved up until that particular time."

The assessments given by Norment and Toan are echoed by Felix Larkin, chairman of W. R. Grace & Company, a multibillion-dollar corporation dealing in chemicals, related natural resources, and selected consumer services.

"There is no question that most phases of business are becoming overregulated. In large measure, it is a factor of the increased size of business units and of labor, and the inadequacies of state, municipal and city governments, all of which cause a large federal government. It is a case of reaction to action."

As we enter a period of reform

No one really expects big government to go away. Most people would not even argue that it should go away. But we are moving into a period of reform; we have to reform those institutions that have been put into place, all to hastily, over the last 45 years and particularly in the last 15 years. Regulation is part of this major issue. It is almost obscene to consider that Americans have to live with more than a million federal and state laws, some 1,500 pages long. Yet on top of that, tens of thousands of pages are issued by government regulatory agencies each year. What may be needed is for the Congress to decide on two or three top priorities, which it will systematically study and act upon during a given year. Whether such a move would ever be possible, however, is extremely debatable.

What do we need for a dynamically growing economy? We first need to curb and slow the growth of government, because the role of government is paracitic. It does not contribute to the nation's productivity nor to its competitive stature in terms of goods, sales, or services. Second, we need tax reform to encourage investment capital accumulation. Third, we need to reexamine all regulations and to do away with those that are no longer needed or perhaps never were needed in order to make industry much more competitive. Finally, along with regulation, we must work even harder than presently to alleviate our two long-term overriding problems of inflation and unemployment.

I. W. Abel, former president of the United Steelworkers of America, views, the "American Way" as the approach to a better tomorrow.

"American society has always held out promises, and the workers of this nation have lived their lives on the assumption that work under our free enterprise system is not only natural and rewarding but also essential to personal survival. . . . Accordingly, they go to school, get married, raise families, take up arms, support huge mortgages, make plans for a brighter future. . . . The American worker has been told over and over again that making himself gainfully useful, through sweat and diligent effort, is the key to economic security and personal progress in our form of society.

"To have that better tomorrow, it will be worthwhile for people in government to have business experience, and people in business to have government experience. I believe there would be a much better understanding of how the whole system works if this were the case. I understand that not everybody can do it, but some leaders should."[4]

Gov. Edmund G. ("Jerry") Brown, Jr., of California sees the problem not so much as one of outsized regulatory policies or of lack of cross-education of people in business and politics. He questions who should have the power and from where the power should be exerted.

"Whether or not we have to require a person who drives a motorcycle to have a helmet on is decided by somebody in Washington. I think that ought to be left to the people of California. If we have a food stamp program, whether we put on a paper clip or whether we staple them comes out of a rule in Washington. . . . I think those decisions ought to be made right in the cities and the states of America. I am talking about a decentralization of power and a slowing down of the growth of government where possible, recognizing that if we don't put this country to work, if we don't preserve the cities of this nation, then the country itself faces a very bleak future. . . .

"I haven't said the federal government shrinks. Government grows. The question is, at what rate of growth, and where are the decisions being made. It's possible to decentralize decisions."[5]

In his analysis of the regulation issue, Prof. George Cabot Lodge of Harvard University put the matter in a more philosophical perspective. According to Lodge, the basic problem is not regulation, per se. It is our refusal, as a society, to recognize that a great deal of government regulation is essential. This is the case because our interrelationships and dependencies, of which both Jerry Brown and Malcolm Denise spoke, are now so extensively developed. The problem is that we have failed to acknowledge this new situation.

"The old idea of the limited state has been supplanted. This has been going on for at least 50 years, with the idea that the state has a planning function. Whether we like it or not, the state, today, is planning. The unfortunate thing about having made this transition without being aware of it is that we have lots of planning, regulation, intervention that is very incoherent. One reason it is incoherent is that we still like to linger romantically with the old idea of the limited state. If we linger with old ideas out of a sort of romantic or mythic affection and, in fact, move to a new idea without doing it explicitly, we get the worst of all possible worlds and our instructions are seen as being illegitimate. There are very few criteria by which managers can judge themselves or be judged because they have left the old ideology; the old one is not clear and so you have a canceling out. This helps explain some of the more obvious characteristics of our time in which managers, in both the public and the private sectors, and deprived of authority, legitimacy, and confidence. This is part of what I see as being the transformation of western civilization."

Dr. Jack D. Steele of the University of Southern California (who served on the National Advisory Board for Small Business) calls attention to the crazy-quilt pattern that he feels characterizes much of the government's regulatory efforts. This characteristic, like the new stringency mentioned earlier by Arthur Toan, Jr., may account in part for the great burdens that businessmen and women feel these efforts impose.

"I would say that government regulation is not too strong. It is too inefficient. Our regulations have been an additive in a mathematical sense. It has not been systemic. In other words, all of our regulation has been an add-on process. We almost never say we no longer need it. The perfect example would be the ICC [Interstate Commerce Commission] with the railroads. In 1887, the Grange Act was needed. But right now, the railroads do not need the same kind of regulation that we have added on trucks and airlines, and yet we still treated them all equally. With the interdependence of the world, economically, politically, and socially, we need regulation. But it should be in terms of what we are now. For example, I understand that concerning food alone there are 17 agencies making decisions as to what is good for us in terms of the end product in food. They are all independent, not coordinated or systemic. I'm not saying we don't need federal regulation in our production of food and what they produce. But I am saying we don't need 17 independent agencies. What we may need is one agency addressing 1980–1999 problems concerning food."

Viewing the regulation situation from the standpoint of a former Attorney General of the United States, Ramsey Clark complements the picture sketched by Steele. He, too, saw the problem as being more complicated than simple overregulation. Adding to the deficiencies of inefficiency, obsolescence, and redundancy, which Steele mentioned, Clark discussed the problems of misguided purposes and even pockets of underregulation.

"There are areas where we clearly overregulated to our great detriment. There are areas where the purpose originally sought by regulation has been subverted; the industry that was to be regulated has, in fact, come to dominate the regulator. When I looked at the proposal of rail lines that came out of the ICC, whether it was a Penn Central or a Pacific Northwest, back in the 60s, I found them to be usually the most uncompetitive combination that could be conceived. Generally, I found the determinative factor to be the interest of the railroads themselves rather than the public interest, which you would assume would best be served by competition. If you have a rail monopoly, your only competition is going to be air, water, and overland buses and trucks. On the other hand, there are areas where regulation is inadequate and effective regulation is needed. I find it imperative that the synthetic chemical drug industry be regulated. There are drugs that are dangerous, very dangerous, And science is discovering more than 100 new drugs a year that can cause injury to humans, even mutations of genes. Just look at thalidomide and you see what can happen. The public cannot protect itself."

The future of regulation

Concerning the developments anticipated in the area of regulation, the respondents reflected some basic differences of opinion. Dean Rusk, former Secretary of State under Presidents Kennedy and Johnson, and currently on the faculty of the University of Georgia Law School, forsees a tapering off of regulatory activities.

"I think that government regulation is going to decrease because government has recognized that the major employer is private enterprise. They also recognize that the government must stimulate certain kinds of employment. Rightfully so, the government is saying to private enterprise that everyone should have an opportunity to work and everyone who has a talent should go forward in the enterprise."

Others are not so sanguine. Arthur Toan calls particular attention to the inertia associated with regulatory enactments.

"I know that once you get regulations, they are not easy to get rid of. I have participated in government on a local level and I know what happens there. I don't imagine that the federal level is going to be any different than the local level."

Arthur R. Taylor, former president of CBS and presently head of his own banking firm, shares Toan's pessimism about changing the patterns of already established regulatory activities.

"I think that a whole body of regulation that grew up, particularly in situations where the public needed to be protected, is not what we are talking about today. The free market has probably forgotten how to operate in most of those areas. There are other regulations, however, that have dynamic effect and that are giving government a bad name; OSHA started out as a very interesting, praiseworthy human endeavor making work safe."

Similarly, Richard Norment believes that, barring some rather significant new developments, the government will not relax its regulatory efforts.

"Despite short-term variations or apparent reverses in the trend, government's natural propensity for increased regulation will continue. European and American experiences for the last two centuries clearly have shown this to be the case. Issues of environment, resources management, international trade, taxation, human resource management, and many others will continue, if not increase in concern. New problems will generate a demand for new answers and the one national vehicle for these answers will most frequently appear to most people to be the federal government. All this points to an increase in government involvement in business, be it pro- or antibusiness. Corporations will have to continue to adopt new and different procedures and techniques to adjust to the shifting realities. And that adjustment on the part of the business community is going to be a very long-term but necessary process."

The "adjustments" Norment mentions do not all, however, have to be on the part of business. In its efforts to make its own "adjustments," the business community may be able to effect some changes in the long-term strategy that government adopts in carrying out its various regulatory activities. These will be explored in the next section, along with some other ideas that have been proposed for altering the government's posture toward regulatory endeavors.

A call for reform

Reform by business

In his attempt to account for what he feels is excessive government regulation, Richard Norment has cited misinformation on the public's part. This misinformation has placed a good deal of misguided and unwarranted pressure on Congress and the bureaucracy to increase their regulatory efforts. One effective way to combat this problem is through a realistic portrayal of the positive actions business continues to take in meeting society's needs and in solving social problems. This, Norment feels, should help undercut the suspicion the public harbors toward business, which results in counterproductive government actions.

"Any change in the approach of business is going to take a long time; there is a natural inertia to all institutions. And it will take even longer for the general public and government to recognize the change in actions and thus become less skeptical about the motivations of business.

"But business will have to change. While the first responsibility of any company will always be to return a profit to its investors, that still leaves significant ground for a greater sensitivity to social needs. Corporations must consciously consider that they are an integral part of a social complex of mutual support systems. Corporate actions can have a positive or negative effect on the social climate, and therefore the business climate, of their communities, be they local, state, or national. Even if some short-term maximization of profits might be diminished, corporations must consider the social implications of their activities, just as we as individuals within the society must. It is quite possible to structure effective business activities that are compatible with both individual corporate needs and those of the socio-economic environment in which they function.

"With this sense of a corporate social responsibility, business can and must participate more actively in a wider range of traditional social concerns. An important link in this process is increased social involvement, increased activism within the community, increased participation in public issues forums, and a basic elevation of public awareness as to what business's function is in our society. Business actions must go beyond the old monologues of economic education programs. They must move to a level of active dialogue and sharing in the resolution of real social problems.

"Once the business community has undertaken an active and functional part in the broader social fabric, beyond the singular role of providing an economic underpinning, two additional changes will occur. First, corporations will have a better perspective of the impact of their actions and the possible contributions they can make to a better society. And second and more important, society in general will also acquire a fuller appreciation of the real and significant functional role that business is playing in shaping almost every aspect of our living environment. It is this improved understanding of business on the part of the public and its government that will mold the attitude and actions taken by them in regulating and influencing the business process."

Norment is not alone in his view that aggressive public information campaigns can assist business organizations in alleviating some of the problems experienced because of government regulation. Another variant of this same strategy emphasizes efforts to educate Congress and the bureaucracy about problems that business and industry must overcome. The Dow Chemical Company has experimented successfully with a program of site visits for legislative and bureaucratic officials to Dow facilities. The purpose of these tours has been to familiarize government personnel with company activities and the specific problems the chemical industry faces. According to R. A. Quigley, a Dow vice-president, this type of on-site exposure of public officials to the problems and operations of his particular business is an attempt to achieve the establishment by the government agencies of "workable rules and regulations . . . based on reason and technology."[6]

The different approaches to solving problems, businessmen feel, have been created in reaction to inappropriate regulations.

Reform by government—national goals

A second set of proposals calls for direct action by Congress to exert greater control over the bureaucracy in its issuance of regulations. Representative Levitas introduced legislation in the 94th Congress and again in the 95th providing for congressional review of regulations prior to their being issued by the executive branch. In a speech accompanying the introduction of three bills on this subject, Levitas called attention to the great impact that regulations can have on the lives of individual citizens.

> Embodied in the principles of the Magna Carta, the Declaration of Independence, the Constitution and its Bill of Rights is the basic tenet that government must be by the consent of the governed and that due process of law is fundamental and essential. Would any American citizen seriously argue that a person should be deprived of liberty or property under decrees which no elected official has participated in promulgating? Yet, today, the fact is that vastly more rules are made by the decree of the unelected bureaucracy than by the elected members of Congress. In most instances, a consequence of violating these administrative rules is imprisonment, or fine, or both.
>
> If you ask the man on the street who makes the law in this country, he would likely tell you that Congress does. But, he would be wrong, because more edicts regulating his life are promulgated by unelected officials than are passed by the elected Congress. An administrative rule is, in effect, a law. It has the same force and effect as a law. A person can go to jail, in many instances, for violating an administrative, bureaucratic rule just the same as if he had violated an act of Congress.[7]

Representative Levitas' bill, which should interest everyone, business representatives included, concerned the wide latitude that Congress gives bureaucrats in establishing regulations. The bill calls for a mandatory 60-day review by Congress of all proposed regulations, during which time the regulations could not take effect. The regulations would then go into effect at the end of the 60 days, unless disapproved by at least one house of Congress during that period. (See HRs 959, 960, and 961 for information on Representative Levitas' efforts during the 94th Congress; also see "Can Congress Control the Regulators?" *Industry Week*, March 29, 1976, pp. 20ff.)

Legislation dealing with some of these same problems has also been introduced in the U.S. Senate by Senators Jacob Javits (R-N.Y.) and James Abourezk (D-S.D.), among others. Former senator Javits' proposals call for the creation of a Congressional Office of Regulatory Oversight, which would review the activities of the regulatory agencies (e.g., the ICC, FPC, CAB) as well as regulations issued by the bureaucracy. Like the Levitas proposals, Senator Javits' bill would provide for congressional veto over regulations deemed inappropriate by the legislative branch.

A third set of proposals, also originating at the highest government levels, calls for a broad-scale review of all phases of the regulation effort. Proposals for such comprehensive assessments were offered by the Ford Administrtion, as well as by Senators Charles Percy (R-Ill.) and Robert Byrd (D-W.Va.). (See Richard E. Cohen, "Out of the Closet, into Debate Regulatory Reform is here to stay," *National Journal,* May 22, 1976, pp. 704–705.) Their objectives are to identify areas in which changes are needed in the government's regulatory programs and to develop recommendations for implementing such changes.

Broad-scale review of current regulatory efforts can create problems for the business community. Two of the respondents, Dr. Karl P. Sauvant and Thornton Bradshaw, made recommendations about dealing with these problems. Dr. Karl P. Sauvant of the United Nations Centre on Transnational Corporations suggests that a number of key issues must be resolved concerning the goals and objectives that the American economy ought to pursue in the coming years. Although he stops short of advocating rigid economic planning, Sauvant is nevertheless convinced that a broad economic policy framework is needed within which the government's regulatory program can be planned and executed. He cites consumer protection as one area in which the government's activities could benefit from the availability of an overall economic policy framework.

"It appears to me that more government guidance is necessary for the economy as a whole. Not a planned economy, but a guided economy, an economy where the partners—in this case, government, business, and labor—work together and set certain target dates, certain marks that could be used for the orientation of all involved. The national management of the economy is becoming more important in order to avoid recessions, in order to avoid any swings that are unacceptable for the country as a whole.

"Beyond that, it appears that at one point, some changes have to occur in business philosophy. There might be changes created within business, or changes that are imposed from above (by government), concerning, in particular, the conservation of resources, the question of style changes, the question of planned obsolesence. In other words, changes might be made in the direction of conserving resources of the country and the world, and to more efficient durable production processes. It has implications in the field of consumer protection, where much could be done. If it isn't being done by government, it won't be done; it has to be done by government. There are areas where future development will occur and is necessary and vital."

Thornton Bradshaw, chairman and chief executive officer of RCA and former president of Atlantic Richfield Co., states, "The lack of clear goals for the United States has brought us into a situation where we pile one regulation upon another. Taken all together, they are counterproductive."[8] He offers ideas similar to Sauvant's for improving the government's regulatory efforts. Like the policy framework suggested by Sauvant, the goals Bradshaw recommends could help introduce order and synthesis among the many diverse, overlapping, and fragmented regulatory endeavors. In a speech before a University of Southern California Commerce Associates dinner, Bradshaw elaborated on these themes, focusing much of the discussion on energy problems. His observations deserve detailed quotation.

"I believe the free market must be preserved—in the case of the oil industry, restored—to prevent the country from fading into a gray state of economic enervation. But I also believe that we cannot be blind to the need for a vigorous government role in the economy as well—setting goals, establishing standards, policing the results, and generally creating a stable but unconstrained environment in which the private sector can accomplish the things we, as a society, decide are needed and wanted.

". . . Where should the government intervene in energy? And what form should the involvement take? The starting place is clearly the establishment of national goals. I've talked about our growing dependence on foreign oil. We still have time to correct this drift *if* the federal government will establish a clear-cut goal for the petroleum industry to pursue and then create a business environment in which its achievement is possible. And that is exactly what I am asking the government to do—to stipulate that, by the middle of the 80s, the United States should be no more than, say, 25 percent dependent for our energy on outside sources, and to establish policies consistent with such a goal. Once that goal is established, the industry can start to adjust its pattern of investment and development to meet it. But if we were to rely entirely on the market to signal investments required to meet energy goals nine years in the future, the signals would come too late.

"It is not that the government is somehow smarter than private entrepreneurs or superior in a philosophical sense. But government *is* obliged to give the country long-range directives and it is positioned to do it. Business is not. Under the broad goal of energy independence, as defined and mandated by the government, there would be a series of *subgoals* for restraining consumption and increasing supplies of oil, gas, coal, nuclear energy, etc. How much demand is anticipated in each area? Then, what kind of incentives, penalties, and capital flow diversions are needed to realize these objectives?

"In the case of offshore oil and gas, for example, it is necessary to establish effective means of protecting the coastline and marine life by means of setting environmental standards to be met by the states, working in cooperation with Washington. The essential thing is that the regulations are standardized throughout the country and not permitted to continue to be subject to regional political whim and prejudice.

"The same applies to coal and nuclear development. The federal government should set rigid standards—again, in conjunction with the states and possibly modeled on good state regulatory plans—to govern development of these resources."[9]

Bradshaw suggests that the government consider other "pressure point intrusions," including a "parallel set of standards for restraining demand. The 55 MPH limit is a start. But we also need mandated mileage for cars, a graduated tax on horsepower, and subsidies to help homeowners insulate their homes."[10] Finally, Bradshaw calls for government-supported research and development efforts directed toward "future fuels." Private industry, he argues, simply cannot mobilize the capital resources necessary for this task.

Like Sauvant, then, Bradshaw feels that the proper regulatory role for the government is to establish economic goals and a variety of performance standards to which business will be held accountable. In this way he hopes that greater rationality and coordination can be introduced into the whole regulatory effort.

Can reform work?

The need for major reform and change in the government's regulatory programs is the only major point on which a consensus is evident among the respondents. Beyond that, disagreements abound. Opinions differ considerably on the nature of the problem (what types of government practices need change), its adverse effects (additional costs, loss of personal and corporate freedom), and the elements of an effective solution. Many of the proposals examined in the course of this discussion offer distinct advantages over others. Yet, no single recommendation satisfactorily addresses all the myriad difficulties associated with the government's present attempts at regulation. Perhaps this is because the problem itself is so large and the issue so complex that it defies any comprehensive remedy.

The proposals that suggest that a congressional presence be injected into the development and implementation of the government's efforts at regulation reflect the feeling that regulatory efforts have gotten out of hand. Representative Levitas' recommendation that Congress review proposed regulation would counteract some of the excessive discretionary power that Levitas believes Congress has surrendered to the bureaucracy. But can one expect Congress, which is already burdened with numerous responsibilities and not renowned for acting expeditiously, to have the time to review meaningfully the great quantity of regulations the bureaucracy issues? Even if Congress has the time to discharge such responsibilities, is it equal to this demanding task? Levitas' proposal for a 60-day review would not effectively address either (a) the huge body of regulations now on the books or (b) the efforts of the regulatory agencies.

The recommendation advanced by Senator Javits to create an Office of Regulatory Oversight is an attempt to address both the activities of the regulatory agencies and the bureaucracy. Moreover, the Javits proposal does offer some op-

portunity for retrospective review of current practice (at least with respect to the regulatory agencies). Senator Javits' recommendations include a
requirement that Congress should give attention
to the projected economic impact of new regulatory
issuances. Everything considered, the economic
analysis envisioned by the Javits proposal is still
too narrow in its scope. It would not provide for
any type of policy framework in which the results
of the analysis could be interpreted. But the very
notion of requiring the economic analysis is in itself highly significant.

The key challenge to businessmen and women
and others concerned about the current chaotic
state of government regulation is to change the
entire process in four major ways. First, regulatory
efforts should focus on, and be consistent with,
larger national economic goals. Second, current
regulatory practices should be examined and,
where necessary modified, to achieve consistency
with the overall policy embraced in those overall
goals. Third, particular regulatory agencies should
be eliminated or modified if their purposes conflict
with those of the overall policy. And fourth, the
new process for conducting regulatory activities
should itself be reviewed and changed if future
developments indicate that such changes are
needed.

Of all the proposals in circulation, those offered
by the Ford Administration (to conduct a systematic industry-by-industry assessment of the impact of the government's regulatory practices) and
Senators Charles Percy and Robert Byrd (to conduct a survey of agency regulatory efforts) deserve
particular attention. The research and analysis
would be immense and would have to be conducted in stages. But a comprehensive survey of
regulatory impact would yield data that could serve
as a basis for developing well-defined national economic goals.

On balance, the Percy/Byrd proposal seems
more workable than the Ford proposal, if only because agencies are more clearly identifiable than

industries. The Ford proposal presents the difficulty of determining what activities and organizations constitute a particular industry. Nevertheless, the Ford and Percy/Byrd proposals both suggest a number of key tasks that must be completed in order to address the issues associated with the present state of government regulation: What is the overall impact of the different regulatory activities? What costs are associated with these outcomes? What possibilities are there for eliminating, combining, or otherwise modifying regulatory activities found to be unjustified?

Regulatory reform: The author's view

How reform might be started

In order to complete successfully the studies required to evaluate overall the government's regulatory policies, Congress will have to mandate the use of a large number of nongovernment research personnel. There are insufficient numbers of such persons (e.g., cost accountants, economists) available through the organizations that normally provide such assistance to Congress, such as congressional staff, the Government Accounting Office, and the Congressional Budget Office. In some instances the various bureaucratic agencies may have greater staff resources. However, enough of these persons would probably not be released from their regular duties for sufficient periods to conduct the required research. In addition, the use of nongovernment researchers would offer greater objectivity and thus enhance the credibility of the research results.

As a first step in defining the scope and content of the assessment, Congress should delineate in detail the objective of the research; that is, the data developed should identify effects as precisely as possible, both fiscal and otherwise, of the current regulatory practices. The monetary effects involved in complying with the various regulatory policies should include the dollar costs incurred by affected organizations, the costs imposed upon consumers/taxpayers, and the costs to the government for enforcement. In addition, the costs associated with the ills regulations are designed to alleviate—for example, the costs to society of the pollution from unregulated auto emissions—should be estimated. Where possible, the nonfinancial effects (e.g., the types of activities restricted or prohibited by the regulations) should also be identified, as should the key groups and population segments effected, if these can in fact be pinpointed within the overall U. S. population.

Rather than attempt to group agencies and organizations into clusters for analysis, Congress should mandate that each Cabinet department, independent bureaucratic agency, and regulatory agency be studied independently. At the conclusion of the data-gathering phase, the results of the separate researchers should be pooled.

When the results of the reviews have been compiled, the regulatory efforts of the different government organizations can be evaluated in terms of the cost and performance data. With this information in hand, Congress will thus be provided a context for evaluation. Departments and agencies will be side by side and in the open, where their relative efficiency or inefficiency will be publicly and quantitatively evident. Congress may then set out to determine which practices seem counterproductive to their originally defined purposes, which impose questionable costs, where duplications are evident, and so forth.

One may certainly object that this procedure requires Congress to beg certain questions, such as the criteria for determining what constitutes excessive costs. At a minimum, it could be argued, these levels and standards ought to be established before the research is complete so that the interpretation of the results is more objective. Ideally, the standards would be preestablished. The reason for recommending another course is that currently no one really knows enough about the impact of the government's regulatory programs to make any sort of intelligent judgments about what levels of regulatory performance are desirable and/or feasible. These sorts of determinations will be possible only after an extensive survey has been conducted and its data compiled.

Just as the data obtained through the survey will allow Congress to judge roughly the performance of the current regulatory process and activities, that same data will aid in establishing goals for the government's future regulatory efforts. These performance standards and levels then can be used to evaluate subsequent regulatory efforts in a way that will raise fewer methodological and procedural disputes.

The references to the future suggest other points that ought to be addressed. It is obvious that the proposals suggested above draw most of their inspiration from the Ford and Percy/Byrd recommendations. However, we should not conclude that little or nothing of value can be appropriated from the other recommendations reviewed. It should be obvious that the emphasis on goal setting drew generously from the comments of Karl Sauvant and Thornton Bradshaw. The cost-benefit considerations certainly owe more than a little to the observations of Henry Duncombe, who wondered whether the government's current regulatory efforts could be justified on economic terms. Finally, the proposals by Representative Levitas and others concerning the need for review of future regulatory efforts are relevant. At the least they suggest that specific provision for review ought to be a major element of any program for improving the government's regulatory efforts.

One method for conducting such reviews without overburdening Congress involves annual congressional committee review. A committee exercising legislative jurisdiction over a particular department, independent bureau, or regulatory agency would hold hearings once a year to allow any person or group aggrieved by any element of a current regulatory effort to come forward and voice his or her complaints. It could be argued that this places too much of a burden on the aggrieved party—that is, he or she ought not to have to bear the major responsibility for pinpointing problems. In addition, it could be argued that some aggrieved parties may be reluctant to come forward; they may fear antagonizing the agency or organization that regulates them.

This objection has validity. Therefore, in addition to the annual hearing, Congress ought to provide for future reviews of the government's overall regulatory posture on the same scale as the all-agency assessment already proposed. In view of the present tendency of the bureaucracy to exert its own independence in regulatory matters, it would be helpful if these periodic reviews occurred frequently—at least once every 10 years, maybe even at lesser intervals.

An active business lobby

A second point concerning the future relates to the need for involvement by the business community in all activities of the Congress. It must not be forgotten that Congress enacts the statutes that establish the regulatory functions undertaken by the bureaucracy and the independent agencies. Congress provides continuing funding for these organizations. And Congress delegates vast rule-making authority to the bureaucracy. Thus, business must not forget that Congress ultimately provides the bureaucracy with the latitude it enjoys in its various regulatory activities.

There is nothing novel in the requirement that business give ongoing attention to congressional activities. Such a requirement has been applied to all segments of society since the founding of the republic and will remain as long as constitutional processes continue. It might be argued that one alternative worth exploring is the enactment of one or more constitutional amendments. Such legislation would forbid government involvement in certain sectors of the economy that are deemed inappropriate sectors for government involvement. Such an approach, however, has many drawbacks. Constitutional amendments are not easily enacted. However, if the comments of those interviewed for this book are at all representative of the business perspective on regulatory matters, government ought to leave particular areas completely and do a more effective job in all those areas of its regulatory involvement.

A guarded prognosis

The role of business vis-à-vis congressional output is likely to remain as it has been in other times. Business will continue to seek all legal and ethical means available to influence that output. This certainly includes efforts to determine the composition of Congress through legitimate support of friendly candidates. In addition, once any given Congress is elected, efforts will continue to provide information to individual members of Congress on legislative alternatives. Business will continue to indicate support or opposition of such alternatives as well as participate in public discussions and debates to which Congress may be attuned.

The crucial consideration concerning the future, however, pertains to the likelihood that Congress cannot really perform all the tasks proposed in this chapter. Congress is often criticized (and justly so) for being too slow in its operation, too parochial in its interests, and too concerned with the present to undertake broad-gauged assessments or reviews of the sort recommended here. Naturally, if Congress is unwilling or unable to proceed along the course suggested, the whole idea of an all-embracing review of regulatory programs becomes impossible. Those who cite the unlikelihood of effective congressional action do so with good cause. However, there are certain indications that Congress may be capable of responding in a less traditional way to the issues of regulation.

The public concern about regulations, particularly the concern voiced by the business community, is so widespread that it cannot be ignored. Moreover, the concern is not limited to a few questions and problems. Rather it cuts across the entire spectrum of government activity. Therefore, Congress cannot hope to solve the problem by a few token gestures. The very diversity of complaints voiced about regulatory activities indicates that such complaints can only be addressed with a comprehensive program.

Congress has already taken a number of steps, some more impressive than others, to deal with the regulation issue. Perhaps congressional interest in the regulation issue can be encouraged and their efforts targeted toward a comprehensive review and the development of a broad-gauged program for the future. To be sure, legislators who have proposed less sweeping solutions may not be easily swayed. Pride of authorship in their own recommendations may interfere or they may not, in principle, accept the idea of dealing with the regulation problem in a comprehensive manner. Nevertheless, these legislators have acknowledged that the problem exists and requires immediate action.

But what if Congress, notwithstanding all the optimistic proposals given in the chapter, still insists on addressing the problems in a partial, piecemeal fashion? Business would then have to act. Some recommendations for business action in less-than-promising environment will be discussed in the next section. It should be noted, however, that these recommendations would also be applicable in a favorable situation, one in which comprehensive solutions to the regulation problem are investigated.

Additional strategies

Unfortunately, the debate concerning regulation has not been characterized by a high degree of clarity and precision. Greater specificity is needed, whether the dialogue takes place as part of a comprehensive effort to address the regulation problem or in connection with attempts to bring about incremental improvements.

The nature and scope of the actual problems that business attributes to regulation form the first cluster of points needing greater precision. Some of the problems the respondents discussed stem from the activities of the regulatory agencies, others from the efforts of the bureaucracy, and still others from the legislative activities of Congress. The term *government regulation* insufficiently describes the many activities that can cause the negative effects the respondents deplored, such as excessive reporting requirements and unnecessary costs. In order to participate effectively in the debate, business must focus sharply on the specific policies, programs, and activities that it wishes to change. It must then offer a convincing rationale for effecting such changes. Such specificity is a key prerequisite to initiating and sustaining a constructive debate.

The contributions that business offers to the dialogue must be solution-oriented. Although, the paucity of current thinking on the regulation issue is such that practically any ideas about solving current problems would enhance the quality of the dialogue, this sad situation in no way justifies our being content with half thought out proposals. Rather, the dearth of rigorous analysis itself makes the requirement for concerted efforts in developing solutions all the more essential.

All the participants in the discussion should be alert for opportunities to upgrade and improve proposed solutions that require greater refinement. For example, Bert Lance, director of the Office of Management and Budget under President Carter, suggested that one way to address the problems he associated with ineffective regulation is for the government simply to issue fewer regulations. This idea may have some visceral appeal to those who see regulation as a daily burden. But it offers no real guidance on how one might address the great variety of difficulties that regulatory efforts may engender.

Suppose fewer regulations are issued. Does this necessarily mean their ill effects will be fewer? Hardly. To be sure, complaints are sometimes voiced about the difficulty in comprehending what a regulation means. But this has more to do with poor writing, poor wording, and jargon than with volume. Rather, it is the activities that regulations mandate that are the chief source of complaint from the business community. The texts of regulations could be rendered with greater brevity and intelligibility yet still sustain, even increase, the level of difficulties such issuances generate.

Nevertheless, with certain modifications, Lance's suggestion could add constructively to our thinking about regulatory issues. If the problem Lance addresses is the burden that regulations impose, then the task is to find mechanisms for reducing those burdens and increasing the benefits that regulation is supposed to provide society. In dealing with a simplistic suggestion such as the one Lance proposed, the responsibility of any participant in the debate on regulation is not to accept it as proposed nor discard it out of hand. Rather the person has a duty to look beyond the limits of the idea itself. Beyond these limits, a rigorous analysis is waiting to be completed. But the entire business community, and anyone else concerned about regulation, can draw inspiration and encouragement from Lance's obvious determination to begin to confront the regulation issue squarely.

A second proposed solution to the regulation quagmire is a suggestion by former President Carter: Cabinet secretaries should be required to read personally all regulations issued by their respective departments. The idea, of course, is to make the Cabinet officials more sensitive to the need for clarity and reasonableness in regulatory provisions. The trouble with President Carter's suggestion is that it suffers from the same basic problem identified in Lance's notion of "fewer regulations." It offers no promise whatsoever of addressing and dealing effectively with the problem it is designed to solve. Clearly, secretarial review of the volume of regulations currently issued is infeasible. "Aha," say the proponents of Mr. Carter's view. "What better way to cut down on such volume?" But as have already noted in dealing with Lance's suggestion, brevity does not guarantee anything positive. Moreover, making regulations briefer, permitting them all to be read by the Cabinet secretaries, could cause new problems. Congress would probably begin to add more bulk to the detail of its statutory enactments. Instead of reducing quantity, an increase in quantity could result. The situation would likely remain as confused as ever. The new sources of confusion would be the only real change.

The thrust of President Carter's suggestion for personal review of proposed regulations was, apparently, to improve quality of such regulations. In turn, that would increase the chances that their impact will benefit the economy more. In assessing such an idea, the business community should attempt to identify how it can contribute to improving such quality and impact. For example, business could devise regulations within a context of larger economic and government goals, or it could provide for a systematic and continuing review of regulations.

The idea of cutting down annual government reporting requirements is another example of a proposal that is inadequate by itself. Nonetheless, it provides a starting point for improvement. This suggestion was proposed by the National Association of Small Businessmen. Two reports would be submitted: an income tax return and a summary of the major characteristics and background of the organization and its operations. Now the Commission on Federal Paperwork estimates that various federal agencies are producing each year 10 billion sheets of forms, applications, and reports at an annual cost to taxpayers of $40 billion. One such form alone, Form 941 of the IRS, costs the government $20 million and the public more than $200 million.

As with the Lance proposal for fewer regulations, this idea is based on sound perceptions about difficulties associated with regulations—in this case, paperwork and "red tape." Nevertheless, merely reducing the number of reports will not necessarily solve anything. Collecting the information required to compile an "all-purpose" report like the one the NASB recommends could conceivably be more burdensome than is currently the case for the several reports businesses must compile and submit.

First, the problem—excessive paperwork—must be addressed and its components identified. Otherwise, *necessary* paperwork may mistakenly come under attack. Then the challenge is to delineate and evaluate the essentials of the proposed solution and to begin to explore how paperwork could be reduced without forgoing benefits, which the government's regulatory efforts do bring about in some instances.

In addition to providing greater precision in its critique of regulation and focusing on a rigorous assessment of proposed solutions, business must also attempt to enlist outside support. Other segments of society can inject their viewpoints, assuring a more broad-based, rational standard in the regulatory efforts. Business is not at all alone in its frustration over many of the government's present regulatory activities. Certainly, the labor community has reason to feel frustrated. Job opportunities may be reduced by inappropriate government involvement in business activities. Those in the social services suffer a great deal of anxiety, uncertainty, resentments, and despair over regulations that conflict with one another, that mandate unnecessary activities, that change continually, and that otherwise hamper the operation of their programs. Similarly, while this may seem incredible, bureaucrats could also profit from a more effective program of regulation. Their jobs would be easier if they did not continually have to interpret and apply confusing, contradictory, and permanently unstable regulations.

The various actions recommended in this section should not be considered in isolation. The pursuit of each can contribute to more effective efforts, with regard to the others. For example, greater precision in naming sources and causes of difficulties associated with regulatory efforts will enhance efforts to develop solutions and promote efforts to rally groups to the cause of regulatory reform. Similarly, reform leaders who are able to express clearly the objectives of their reform proposals will enjoy greater credibility, which will aid them in coalition building. The ability to express one's views and the credibility associated with it are possible only if one has thoroughly analyzed and documented their case for change.

As indicated at the end of the preceding section, these recommendations are applicable whether comprehensive reform efforts are being undertaken or only piecemeal, incremental solutions are possible. Even in the latter circumstances, precision in debate, thorough analysis of proposed solutions, and coalition building can all help promote a situation in which more comprehensive reform is possible.

Can we look to new challenges?

This chapter has provided an overview of the current scene. We must, however, look beyond the present to the remainder of the 1980s—and the 1990s—a time not far away—when new challenges and opportunities will confront the U. S. economy and the business community. What is likely to occur in years to come? What will the nature and shape of the government's regulatory program be in the next decade? I have attempted to sketch a situation that I think ought to prevail—that the government, with Congress taking the lead, ought to begin a systematic and comprehensive evaluation of the regulation program so that the program can meet the requirements that the 1980s and 90s will impose. But will this program or a similar one be undertaken? Will

Congress or some other body attempt instead to implement less comprehensive reform? Or will the situation remain much as it is today, with a great deal of discussion (albeit a discussion involving intense thought and analysis) but little effective action to correct current problems?

If the respondents' comments and the written sources consulted are any indication, no one seems to expect any drastic change, either for better or worse, in the current program of government regulation. To be sure, all the intense debate that has surrounded the issue to this point will probably result in some actions. Some form of congressional oversight of the regulatory process will probably be established. The bureaucracy and the regulatory agencies will likely be asked to offer judgments about the sector(s) of the economy for which they bear a statutory responsibility. Nevertheless, none of the respondents offered any reason to expect that these changes will be along the lines of the comprehensive reform proposals promoted in this book. Nor do the respondents expect that any changes that do occur will avoid the pitfalls that have been identified.

In response to this rather dour prediction, I would like to offer a few final comments. First, although there are no signs that anyone is prepared to come to grips with the basics of the regulation problem, a lack of signs is no cause in itself to despair. Indeed, the absence of any positive indications that fundamental changes are afoot may be a blessing of sorts. It may cause those concerned about regulation-related issues to redouble their efforts.

Second is an observation that I can take only scant comfort in making. Even barring the development of the comprehensive critique and assessment of the U. S. Government's current regulatory program, steps can be taken (including several mentioned in this book) that may help affect some marginal improvements in the situation. It has been repeatedly noted that these improvements would be more effective in the context of a broad-scale attack on the regulation issue. Nevertheless, piecemeal improvements are preferable to no improvements. Thus, if an all-out assualt on the problem is not feasible due to the political impediments or to lack of interest on the part of the business community or other natural proponents of the idea, some guerilla warfare around the edges of the issue is still possible.

Finally—and again no real satisfaction is derived from this conclusion—the failure to address the regulation question in any of the ways recommended will not send the U. S. economy tumbling into ruin. The American economy is the largest and one of the strongest on earth, and the United States is one of the truly dominant global forces of the 20th century. The American economy is extremely tough. It has prevailed against many previous challenges and is sustaining itself and continuing to grow despite all the impediments created by the current system of regulation.

The tragedy of continuing with "regulation as usual" is not that such a policy will plunge us into the abyss. It won't. Rather, it will mean that opportunities for greater productivity, for developing better means of dealing with such pressing problems as dwindling sources of natural energy, for helping Third World countries address their economic challenges will be reduced. Hence, a substantial portion of the problem-solving potential that the U.S. economy could offer in the 1980s and 90s will be needlessly wasted.

The late Dr. Margaret Mead, author and curator emeritus of enthnology at the American Museum of Natural History, understood this problem. She saw its roots in human nature. In an article in *Business and Society Reviews*, Mead stated the following.

> Traditionally, we have been able to pull ourselves together and suppress our individualism in wartime. I believe that in peacetime it is too much individualism, rather than mere selfishness or profit-seeking or institutional perpetuation, that has been to blame. In World War II, the Seabees

could boast: 'The difficult we do immediately. The impossible takes a little longer.' Can the present dangers from nuclear power, from a polluted environment, from a threatened atmosphere, from a disorganized but interdependent world, be so phrased that we will be able to do real social accounting and be willing to pay today for the good of tomorrow?

2

Community problem solving: The role of business

This chapter addresses key issues that have emerged in the course of the debate over corporate social responsibility. The debate centers on the question: Do business organizations have an ethical obligation to help society solve problems such as environmental degradation, urban decay, and economic deprivation among disadvantaged groups? Certain responsibilities already exist in these areas, of course. They have been imposed by various legal requirements mandating such practices as nondiscrimination in employment and affirmative action. Some commentators, however, feel that businesses are obligated to go beyond mere compliance with the law. A number of activities that a business might voluntarily undertake to help solve social problems have been suggested. Our exploration of the question of corporate social responsibility begins by examining observations that the respondents have offered concerning the overall challenge this issue poses for business organizations. Next is a review of definitional problems. A survey of differing views on what constitutes social responsibility follows. And the chapter concludes with a discussion of factors that limit the capacity of business corporations to address social problems effectively and with my own conclusions about the social responsibility question.

Inducements to socially responsible action

Several respondents have offered comments and observations urging businesses, willingly and voluntarily, to help government and community institutions grapple with problems such as unemployment among ghetto youth. Former Commerce Secretary Juanita Kreps feels that corporations have a strong self-interest in such efforts.

"Corporations understand well that, in the long run, demonstrating responsibility towards society is not a choice but a requisite. Corporate managers today must live with hundreds of externally imposed rules and regulations. Many of these rules govern aspects of corporate behavior that managers in an earlier time regarded as private and discretionary. Had these managers understood that their authority to determine their behavior ultimately depended on how the behavior accorded with the interest of their constituents, many of these regulations today would not exist."[1]

The views of Georgia state senator Julian Bond on the changing nature of protest patterns in the United States are also relevant to the issue of business and its responsiveness to new community forces and problems.

"The 1960s were a time of coerciveness, a time of violence, a time of pressure, a time that was often unsophisticated. The 1970s are to be remembered as a period for planning, a time to become aggressive and knowledgable in a professional, nonviolent, academic way. The 1980s will be an awakening period, a time of positive, nonviolent resistance. But it will be aggressive and professional. People will knock on the doors of institutions and present themselves and their reasons for being there.

"The 1980s will be a time when men and women will be more equal, presenting themselves for the same cause. The 1980s will be a time when institutions will, more than ever before, have to govern themselves accordingly. The concept of Big Brother will now be a part of a more sophisticated and more informed society composed of people who will together, as one, guide and monitor those selfish institutions that still feel they should only provide for themselves.

"The 1980s should be a period of great change, of great transformation. Institutions will no longer be able to function under the philosophy and concept of profitability alone. It cannot be denied that the survival of many institutions is based on an adequate cash flow. But the awakening of peoples, the awakening of our society, will dictate that all institutions must be governed by a sense of human satisfaction not found in many of our institutions today. No longer can our businesses or our unions be dictated by those small groups of individuals who profess loyalty to the concept of fairness and human dignity, and create a final product that smells of immoral conduct and dignity lacking totally in the importance of truth and fairness."

It is obvious that, in the remaining part of this century, society will demand more from its institutions in general and from its business corporations in particular. Senator Bond predicts that the 1980s will be "a period of great change, of great transformation." His comments alert us to the fact that business organizations will have to continue to respond to the exhortations of various groups demanding more intense involvement in social problemsolving. In that regard, Bond's remarks are relevant and his fervor welcome. Similarly, Secretary Kreps' analysis of the relation between socially responsible behavior and regulation may be oversimplified. Nevertheless, she is absolutely correct in urging business leaders to be attentive to the needs of various constituents, if for no other reason than that further government regulations may be forestalled as a result.

Dr. Henry Duncombe, former chief economist at General Motors, has raised similar issues about the nature of the demands to which the business community must respond. According to Duncombe, a business concern must do more than just keep the customer satisfied.

"The role of government in economic and personal affairs has undergone vast expansion. We do have new values that are largely being implemented by government—the increased social concern with the improvement of the environment and the future of the central city, and the increased personal concern of a great number of people about what they are doing with their lives. These concerns are being reflected in the new demands that are being put on government and business. A business is concerned with producing and selling something it will have a buyer for. By and large its efforts are almost single-handedly directed towards satisfying the customer. What society has been telling us is that it is necessary for business to satisfy more than the demands of the individual customer."

The need for business organizations to act in a socially responsible manner is not really at issue. However, if corporate social responsibility is going to be part of the cost of doing business and is going to be included in the cost of goods sold, then how does a corporation know when it is acting responsibly? How does it know what to do in order to be socially responsible?

Corporate social responsibility: What does it mean?

It is obvious that the business community is going to be asked to take a much more positive role in the areas of social and community development than in the past. Increasingly, corporations will have to be concerned with issues such as poverty, discrimination, job safety, and the environment. The business leaders of the future will have to be more conscious of, and sensitive to, these political and social issues. They will have to ask themselves more forcefully than in the past how they can make a social contribution that will still be compatible with the need to satisfy and serve the customer, the stockholder, and the community.

Yet the types of contributions that business is expected to make, as well as the scope and breadth of these contributions, are far from clear. This is a point Prof. George Cabot Lodge of Harvard University addresses in his discussion of corporate wrongdoing and social responsibility.

"One of the sources of corporate corruption today is the vague, inconsistent, contradictory set of criteria the community sets. The responsibility of a large corporation, or any corporation, is without question set down by the community in which it operates. That responsibility must be sharpened and clarified. I would hope that, in the clarification, the efficiency of the corporation will not be damaged. Efficiency is a value; it is noncontroversial. There again, it becomes desirable for the terms of efficiency to be clearly defined; the manager and the corporation do better, have more authoritative lives, and have more legitimacy to the extent that the parameters are clear within the area in which they operate."

In the view of Arthur B. Toan, Jr., formerly of Price Waterhouse, social responsibility consists of two parts.

"The first part is the definition of the items of social concern, the set of factors that are to be considered in determining the social responsibilities of a corporation or its social performance. The second part is the determination of what constitutes responsible social performance."

On the abstract level, there is considerable agreement among business leaders, politicians, and the public about preferred social values. This consensus rapidly dissolves, however, when the discussion turns to specific problems. The next section will focus on a number of these specific questions as we examine the differing views the respondents offered about what actually constitutes socially responsible behavior on the part of business organizations.

The challenge business faces

Given the complexity of the corporate social responsibility issue, no one should expect a consensus on this question. Some of the respondents do achieve limited agreement on certain points. Nonetheless, their comments give the unmistakable impression that no consensus is likely to emerge in the near future.

In offering their opinions on corporate social responsibility, several of the commentators sought to highlight their perspectives on the present and future situations by refering to the past. In the case of Irving Shapiro (former chairman of E.I. du Pont de Nemours), the purpose was to underscore what he feels should be the *continuity* between past and present.

"What the primary role of business in society should be in the future is easy to define. It should be exactly what it has been in the past—the provision of goods and services of the highest possible quality, to the largest possible number of people, at the lowest possible prices, which in return create sufficient jobs and reasonable profits."[2]

Shapiro is, however, far from certain that his views on the "correct" understanding of corporate social responsibility will prevail.

"What the future role of business in society actually *will* be is an entirely different question from what it *should* be. My conviction is that the actual future role of business in society cannot be precisely charted today. It will depend to a major degree on how this generation of business management performs and how the public and government react to this performance."[3]

Other commentators also called attention to the contrast between past situations and those of the present and future. Richard Norment of the National Association of Manufacturers, believes that recent social changes require responsive change on the part of business corporations. He suggests that there has to be an increasing involvement on the part of these institutions and a sincere commitment to the realization that they can positively affect the social environment, and therefore the business environment as well. It stands to reason that, if our cities and society are disrupted, business will be equally effected. There are a whole series of social concerns that a corporation can enter into legitimately as part of its relationship with the general community. It will have to become more actively involved, become an active citizen, and take on the same role as any other citizen within a community. Why should a corporation do this? First, Norment argues, it is in its self-interest. Second, it has the resources and ability frequently to solve problems that government cannot. And third, it is a logical focal point for leadership within its community. Norment concludes with this assessment.

"Corporations are going to have to adapt with different procedures and techniques to adjust to the different realities of a changing world. The adjustment on the part of the business community is going to be a very long-term process. And it will take an even longer time for the general public and government to recognize this change of approach and become less skeptical about the role of business."

In his assessment of the social responsibility

problem, Keizo Saji, chairman of the board and president of Suntory Limited of Japan, confines his comments to the present situation. Yet the thrust of his remarks are quite similar to those of Irving Shapiro.

"The role of business in society should be identified by its function to improve the economic welfare of people through development of the economy; the social responsibility of business should be to maximize social utility through the process of converting social resources into economic values. Business profits may be defined as social surpluses, generated by businesses. They are necessary for the accumulation of capital goods and for the achievement of better social welfare. They are, in turn, resources for economic development. In this vein, *a business is no longer socially responsible when it stops seeking profits*, as then there will be less resources available for economic development and efficiency."

Put more bluntly, the social responsibility of business, according to Saji, is to pursue its endeavors in a profitable manner. The use of these profits in promoting business expansion will help assure social betterment.

Similar thoughts are offered by Robert E. Sibson of Sibson and Associates, a compensation consulting firm.

"The whole topic and concept of social responsibility has been an interesting diversion, but most of what has been written and said has simply been a lot of rhetoric. If business is conducted within the letter and spirit of the law, is operated according to the rules of the game laid down by government agencies, and is conducted effectively, then hasn't business met its social responsibilities?"

Sibson thus casts his lot with the more traditional and restrictive view of corporate social responsibility reflected by Shapiro and Saji. Dr. Paul

W. McCracken, former economic adviser to President Nixon, takes a position similar to these commentators. His starting point, however, is somewhat different. He identifies what he feels is the most pressing requirement for social change in modern American society. Then he suggests that the business community can meet these needs by performing its traditional function.

"The great problem with our sociopolitical system tends to respond to social needs and responsibilities only in terms of actions within the public sector. The most fundamental contribution to social needs is a rise in per capita income and our economic system has demonstrated a great capability to deliver that."

The divisions of opinion explored thus far have largely focused on the domestic arena. Certainly, the activist views presented in the discussion of the "challenge" of social responsibility have emphasized contemporary problems affecting American society. The perspectives explored in this section have stressed domestic issues. Andrew Young, former Ambassador to the United Nations, sees the issue of corporate social responsibility through a wider lens, which focuses on the world view. His views are of particular interest because he recommends a definite role for business in helping implement this country's foreign policy.

"On a federal level, especially in the area of international affairs, we are going to have to make a lot more use of the social responsibility of the private sector to have a coherent foreign policy. For instance, there are not many military options for the United States any longer. Foreign policy is going to be a matter of economic competition more than military confrontation. We are going to have to establish some sort of common thinking about investment. Instead of corporations going off completely on their own, there should be some government support, at least a method of gathering research and making long-range projections about how the national interests might best be served through private investment. This could be done by an expanded role for an agency such as the former Council on International Economic Policy. It could even be done by a new vehicle altogether."

In assessing these various suggestions about the proper role of business in solving social problems, I find it difficult to accept wholeheartedly the "restricted" or more "traditional" views. Clearly, business organizations must sustain enough profits to attract investors, replace outmoded equipment, and expand operations when circumstances warrant. If individual organizations fail to meet these and other basic business requirements, their capacity to deal with any issues or contemporary social problems will be short-lived indeed. Nevertheless, after all this is said, the fact remains that the 1980s will likely witness little, if any, reduction of the pressure business leaders now experience. They will continue to be told by various groups to involve themselves and their organizations in addressing social issues. The business community must therefore either respond in some fashion to these continuing calls for action, either by accepting the call or by preparing to argue convincingly why it should not act. I believe that business will have no realistic chance to avoid an ongoing, voluntary role in social problem solving without appearing indifferent or preoccupied with selfish concerns. Surely, the argument that the need to enlarge capital resources precludes investment in recruiting and training the disadvantaged will strike many observers as self-serving and hypocritical.

Beyond the practical considerations, however, there are a host of moral and ethical considerations. They cry out against the notion that business has no social obligations beyond staying solvent and obeying the law, as essential as both obviously are. Like other major community institutions, business organizations must accept significant responsibilities. They helped to create and sustain many of the problems; they should accept the call of advocates of corporate social responsibility who say that the business community should help overcome these problems.

The business communities possess unique skills and resources. In such areas as the fight against environment decay and helping "unemployable" persons find a place in the world of work, no other institution can supply the skills and resources business supplies. The history of the past four decades conclusively demonstrates that government lacks the capacity to overcome major social problems without substantial assistance from other sectors of the community. Business, along with voluntary social service organizations, churches, and civic groups, has a special contribution to make in supporting and complementing government programs. It is as morally indefensible for business to withhold its unique contributions as for any other member of the community to pass up opportunities for active involvement in social problem solving.

It is not within the capacity of the business community to resolve society's many problems by itself. There are major limitations that business organizations face in their efforts to operate as socially responsible members of their communities. The next section will cite and assess some of these limitations. This will be followed by suggestions in the final section of this chapter of a number of positive actions business can undertake in support of community problem-solving efforts.

The need for guidance and direction

Business and business leaders face many limitations, which restrict their capacity to help overcome social problems. Some of these (e.g., the fundamental need to remain profitable) have already been discussed. One of the most serious limitations, and one that has not yet been examined, is the inability of either individual firms or groups of business organizations to establish an authoritative nationwide problem-solving agenda. Business cannot definitively determine which problems require priority attention. Nor can it effectively assign responsibility to the various participants for different aspects of the problem-solving program. These limitations are inherent in the position of business; it is only one among a number of community institutions and lacks real authority to take a leadership role in any joint effort with other institutions.

To be sure, no single institution or group of institutions can assume a leadership role in a way that all other members of the community will find satisfactory. Nevertheless, some type of authoritative agenda setting is needed, if only to provide context and direction for those individuals and groups who are willing to help tackle pressing problems. In the view of Prof. George Cabot Lodge, the government must play the leadership role in this connection.

"Most of the large problems we have are public problems. They involve control and delicate trade-offs that only the political order has the authority to make. The individual businessman has neither the right nor the competence to decide many of these items. The business sector has got to urge, spur, assist, and encourage the political order from the city, to the state, to Washington. Business must make sure that the government leads effectively and efficiently. Then business must serve the needs that have been defined in the most efficient way. We have no shortage of crisis today; the problem is only worsened because the crisis has not been defined, the needs have not been made explicit. This is not an advocacy of or for a big state. If the state did what it has to do, it could be much smaller."

Just as business lacks the capacity to determine problem-solving priorities on behalf of the community, likewise it is restricted in establishing indicators of success. Those institutions, including businesses, that are being asked to offer volunteer assistance in grappling with community problems have a right to demand guidance about how to measure progress. Indicators recommended by government agencies will certainly not enjoy universal acceptance. Yet, because government presumably speaks for a wider community interest than do other institutions, the goals and measures of progress that it suggests will probably command the greatest support.

Business does not entirely lack the technical capacity to conduct periodic assessments of how well its voluntary problem-solving efforts are proceeding. But such determinations are best left to government institutions. Once again, this is because government is equipped to take a broader view of social change than are other community groups and organizations. In addition, government can interpret those changes convincingly. Moreover, the indicators used to gauge progress (or the lack of it) may at times suggest that problem-solving strategies must be altered to deal with changing situations. For the reasons already discussed, government probably stands the best chance of recommending strategy changes that the other community groups and institutions will accept.

Stepping forward toward greater responsibility

Business must voluntarily accept major responsibility for helping solve social problems. However, neither business nor any other community institution can play an effective role in this respect without clear and explicit leadership on the part of government, particularly at the national level. In some fashion, the President and Congress must jointly identify the problem areas most urgently needing increased help and those areas in which additional voluntary help from the private sector would be most appropriate.

Similarly, government must give at least some general guidance. It must suggest the types of service business (or any other community institution, for that matter) ought to render in connection with these pressing problems and how that assistance is to be evaluated. This is not to suggest that business must wait passively until government elects to provide guidance. Left to itself, government will probably remain silent on this issue; at least it will if its past performance is any guide. Business can and must take a number of actions that encourage government to furnish the necessary leadership and to stimulate maximum business community participation in social problem solving. These actions include the following.

1. Business must explicitly acknowledge its willingness to accept a greater responsibility in social problem solving. This will serve to induce government to make sure that proper leadership and guidance is provided. Moreover, should government institutions be slow to respond (as they probably will), the explicit commitment by the business community to become more involved in problem-solving efforts will strengthen its hand in pressuring government to act.

In making this commitment, business must pledge itself to deal with the sorts of questions and issues that concern organizations of all types—hiring the "unemployable," affirmative action on behalf of victims of past discrimination, etc. Business must deal with those specific problem areas in which individual firms may be able to make special contributions. For example, automobile or aircraft manufacturers might undertake additional research into noise or air pollution abatement. Firms in the chemical industry might increase efforts to deal with water pollution, real estate developers with poor land use, and so forth.

Cynics may dismiss these suggestions as wildly unrealistic. They may argue that firms that have contributed to the development of problems will not voluntarily contribute to their solution. These critics may be right. However, I contend that business has both the right and responsibility to bring its special expertise to bear on community problems. Furthermore, business must be challenged to use that expertise to the maximum extent.

2.   Individual firms must actively promote involvement in problem-solving activities by firms that are reluctant to join the effort. The whole matter of social problem solving is extremely important. Individual organizations should not content themselves with merely being responsible for their own participation. The entire business community must be mobilized, if possible. This will expand the resources available and add to the pressure on government to offer the requisite leadership.

3.   Business leaders must be willing to assist government agencies in identifying the specific problems, assigning priorities, and determining use of business resources. This is not suggested to retract in any way the suggestions about the need for overall leadership by government. It does mean that the government, as the only available leader and catalyst for the effort I propose, needs advice and suggestions from a variety of sources, including the business community.

How much time, money, and managerial talent should a business invest in these voluntary activities? This is a judgment for which individual firms must be responsible. Certainly, the financial situation of the organization and the extent of its current involvement in community service will be important factors, which the firm's managers must consider when making such decisions.

In commenting on the current role of U.S. business in promoting community betterment, Elliott Richardson, who has held numerous high-level posts in both the private and public sectors (including four Cabinet positions in the Nixon and Ford Administrations), raised the following question. "Can a corporation be governed by the desire to maximize profit and, through that principle, arrive at good working conditions, good products, and a decent environment?"[4]

My assessment and many of the comments of the respondents indicate that Richardson's question should be answered in the affirmative. But a caveat must be added, stating that the issue should be considered in broader terms. Certainly, businesses can and have achieved profitability while at the same time promoting good working conditions, good products, and a decent environment. Nevertheless, as desirable as those particular goals obviously are, they do not comprehensively describe the numerous other social problems business must be willing to help overcome.

Businesses are full members of both the community in which they are located and the national community. As such, individual businesses are responsible for, and affected by, the full range of social concerns that keep our communities from being as wholesome, safe, and productive as we all desire. Therefore, business must become directly and permanently involved in helping find solutions to vexing problems, such as urban blight, suburban sprawl, unemployment among ghetto youth, and drug and alcohol abuse.

This is not an obligation that has been imposed on business by legislation, government regulation, or any other legally mandated requirement. Rather, the obligations are moral and ethical in nature. They stem from the responsibility that we all bear individually and corporately to recompense the community for the many benefits it confers. We must attempt to play a substantive and continuous role in helping resolve the pressing problems the community confronts.

Legally, of course, a business is in many ways a sovereign economic entity. Yet it is also a subsystem, constantly interacting with society. Therefore, business should always identify itself with society, of which it is an integral part, assuming duties and making contributions as a member citizen. Then and only then may it expect to find its citizenship accepted by society.

3

Multinationals

Like many other subjects discussed by the respondents, the topic of multinational corporations (MNCs) is both controversial and complex. Moreover, the "question" of the multinational corporation is not really a question at all. Rather it is a category of questions in which are clustered a host of more specific problems. These problems include (1) the definition of the MNC, (2) the need (or lack of need) for greater control over the activities of multinational corporations, (3) the types of controls that will be most effective (assuming that additional controls are, in fact, necessary), (4) the contributions MNCs make to economic and social betterment, (5) the most effective way(s) to increase those contributions, and (6) the prospects for MNCs in the near future. This is not an exhaustive list, but it does indicate the range of issues and problems associated with the MNC phenomenon.

In assessing the observations offered by the respondents on various subjects related to MNCs we will begin with definitional problems. In the discussion of the free enterprise system, there was a great need for increased clarity on all our parts about what "free enterprise" means. There was also a need for definitional precision concerning corporate social responsibility. Similar clarity is needed concerning the multinational corporation. Moreover, as is not the case for the other subjects, this requirement is widely accepted by students and commentators with regard to MNCs.

It is only after an analysis of the definitional issue that the discussion can shift to the question of the overall impact of multinationals. The foundation is then set to address questions of how MNC performance can be improved and what the prospects for MNCs may be in the coming decade.

Quest for a definition

In the course of being interviewed, Donald M. Kendall, chairman of the board of PepsiCo, noted that a number of key questions are being raised about multinational corporations. This inquiry is part of a new and increasingly intense interest in the whole subject of multinationals.

"Questions are being directed at such immediate and practical subjects as how the foreign investments of American companies affect American employment and U.S. balances of trade and payments. Basic questions are also being asked, such as: What is a multinational corporation? How did it come about? And even, who needs it?"

The emergence of the MNC will not be given extensive treatment in this discussion, although references are certainly available for the interested reader.[1] The "Who needs it?" issue will be explored as part of the discussion of the performance and future of multinational corporations. At this point, the issue of what constitutes a multinational corporation must be addressed.

Students of the multinational corporation are greatly divided as to what an organization has to do, be, or become in order to qualify for the "MNC" designation. Those interviewed for this book did not devote their undivided attention to developing or recommending specific definitions. However, Prof. Thomas Masterson of Emory University did suggest that a "multinational corporation is a member of 30 or 40 different communities." This is a notion that at least some of those active in research on MNC-related questions would find acceptable. For example, Jacques C. Maisonrouge of IBM suggested, "In order to be truly multinational in character, an organization must operate in a variety of different countries."[2] One should not suppose, however, that there is a generally accepted definition that firmly states that MNCs are necessarily characterized by many complex relationships. In contrast to the complex view, United Nations commentators argue, "A multinational corporation is a business organization which merely operates in more than one country."[3]

The criterion of complexity is merely the start of the definitional argument concerning MNCs. There are other competing concepts available for consideration. Maisonrouge also referred to the definition recommended by Sidney E. Rolfe who has worked for the International Chamber of Commerce. Rolfe holds that an organization must conduct at least 25 percent of its sales, investment, production, or employment operations abroad to attain multinational status.[4]

In addition, Maisonrouge cited the definition that Raymond Vernon offered concerning the multinational corporation. (Vernon, who is currently at Harvard University, is considered the "pope" in the field of multinationals.) According to Vernon, such an organization must operate on a wide geographic scale. All units must be able to draw on a central organizational source for monetary support and for personnel. Furthermore, the size of the organization is also significant. Vernon set

$100 million in sales as the minimum volume an organization must achieve in order to warrant the "multinational" designation.[5]

Peter Vale, another commentator sensitive to the question of definitions, called attention to a series of distinctions among different types of business organizations. Included among these distinctions are those concerning MNCs that were offered by Richard Robinson, head of the Sloan School of Management at MIT. In Robinson's view, the characteristic feature of the multinational corporation is the parity in corporate resource allocation that the organizational components enjoy, regardless of their geographic location. Thus, for Robinson, the multinational firm is one that makes its business policies and decisions "without regard to national frontiers."[6] With these numerous definitions competing for adherence, it should be no surprise that Donald Kendall felt compelled to ask what a multinational corporation is or that Vale had to argue that an adequate definition has not yet been developed.[7]

There is little evidence to suggest that students of multinational corporations or the leaders of these organizations are about to agree on a single, all-purpose definition. Nor are there any easy remedies that can be suggested with the confidence that their adoption will promote effective consensus about such a definition. There are, however, certain actions that may at least help limit the uncertainty and confusion brought on by the many definitions currently in use.

The first recommendation is that all participants in the ongoing debates about multinational corporations should continue to remind each other of the lack of consensus about definitions. They must frequently mention the potential dangers such lack of agreement may pose. This will keep all those concerned with multinational business organizations alert to the need for a greater common understanding about the meaning of the basic concept.

Second, the participants in the debates should explicitly refer to their own particular definition of MNC as part of any pronouncements they may offer on questions related to MNCs. This will make the dialogue more intelligible. It will also, once again, remind the participants of the absence of consensus on the definition issue.

The final suggestion concerns the work being done in a number of forums—for example, the United Nations and the Organization for Economic Cooperation and Development. Although their work to establish acceptable codes of conduct for multinational corporations is deficient in many ways, these activities merit the support and encouragement of business. Code development efforts afford opportunities to push for equitable, effective norms of corporate behavior. However, any norms that emerge from these deliberations will be of little value unless the organizations to which the norms are to apply are defined clearly and rationally.

The impact of MNCs

This portion of the discussion will be brief because the respondents dealt mostly with individual problems and with solutions to specific problems relating to multinational corporations. They did not dwell on generalized assessments. Nevertheless, the comments included in this section provide a useful background for the more detailed analyses that follow.

Georgia state senator Julian Bond enjoys a justifiable reputation as a crusader for social reform and a spokesman for the disadvantaged, both in this country and elsewhere. His attitude toward the multinational corporation is one of considerable wariness and caution.

"I am frightened by the immense power of the multinational corporation. I've read some statistics that estimate that within three years, 50 percent of all the world's goods and services would be produced by multinational corporations. Their ability to shift capital across national boundries and to affect seriously the economy of a host country simply because of profits or losses in some corporate headquarters located somewhere outside the boundaries of the country is a frightening spector."

On the positive side, the capacity of large, well-organized, and well-managed companies to provide benefits to a variety of constituents has not escaped the notice of some of the commentators. D.W. Brooks, chairman of the board of Gold Kist, Inc., feels that the unfavorable publicity some multinational corporations have recently engendered reflects unfairly on the vast majority of such entities.

"Of course multinational corporations have come under great criticism in recent years. Unfortunately, there are a few multinationals that do immoral things. When you do something immoral you give a black eye to the whole industry. But it would be a horrible mistake to say that because one multinational did something wrong or made a mistake they are therefore all wrong. I think that most multinationals have tremendously improved the living standards of the peoples of the world. The one thing that moves people upwards is, of course, knowledge. The multinationals have been in the unusual position of being able to bring in people with great ability."

In his comments, Donald Kendall also celebrated what he feels to be the salutary impact and influence of the multinational corporation. His observations are offered by way of a self-formulated response to a question he had raised earlier.

"The third question I mentioned as being raised about the multinational corporation is 'Who needs it?' The answer to that seems to me to be just about everybody. Because of the uneven distribution of natural resources, such as oil, chrome and bauxite, as well as the vagaries of climate throughout the world, no modern nation can be self-sufficient. America's awakening to the international scarcity of energy should bring to an end any lingering thoughts of insularity in our nation."

A similar view is voiced by former Secretary of State Henry A. Kissinger, who argues that multinational firms can be "powerful engines for good." Kissinger expands on this thesis with the following observations.

> Multinational corporations . . . can marshal and organize the resources of capital, initiative, research, technology, and markets in ways which vastly increase production and growth. If an international consensus on the proper role and responsibilities of these enterprises could be reached, their vital contribution to the world economy could be further expanded.[8]

So strong are Kissinger's convictions about the positive impact of multinationals that he argues at one point, "The controversy over their role and conduct is itself an obstacle to economic development."[9] Perhaps this is true. But it seems more plausible to view the debate about MNCs, heated and strident though it may sometimes be, as helpful both in pinpointing defects in the current system of "multinational enterprise" (a phrase Kissinger sometimes uses) and in developing solutions for those defects.

A positive view of multinationals, similar in some respects to those of Kissinger and Brooks, is advanced by Rawleigh Warner, Jr., chariman of the board of the Mobil Oil Corporation. Warner feels that multinationals offer a healthy and natural response to the economic interdependence that is so characteristic of the modern age.

"There are some in Washington who seem to believe it is good politics to attack multinational corporations as a sinister force. Contrary to their views, however, history will show that, while nations have long struggled to control their own destiny, they are dependent on the international trade that binds them together. The advance of world trade has thoroughly broken down the old concepts of sovereignty. What we now see almost everywhere is a degree of interdependence that is inconsistent with the kinds of barriers with which most nations have tried to surround themselves at one time or another."[10]

Along a somewhat different though related line, Walter B. Gerken, chairman of the board of Pacific Mutual Life Insurance Company, suggests that multinational corporations can assist in promoting goodwill and international harmony. In his view, the benefits associated with the activities of the MNCs extend beyond the economic and material blessings referred to by previous interviewees. He argues that multinationals can help reduce the possibility of war, a goal that has continually eluded politicians over the centuries.

"Multinational companies are a logical extension of the economic development of the world. It has always been my view that one of the basic causes of tension in the world, and the wars that have ensued, has come about from excess nationalism and nationalistic feelings. I have always been a free trader. It makes the most sense for the benefit of all the people of the world to have free trade. A logical extension of the free trade concept is the multinational corporation. It can bring in the managerial skills and the resources that cut across national boundaries, accomplishing a job that ends up benefiting the world. Moreover, it may, over 50 to 100 years, be the device to lessen nationalistic feelings to the point where we may enjoy more of a world order and a world economy—in the truer sense of the word."

Former Secretary of Commerce Juanita Kreps has offered thoughts on the subject of economic interdependence, which are worth quoting at length. Her remarks were offered as part of a discussion focusing on "the new economic realities" that the Carter Administration confronted when it took office in January 1977.

"The first new reality was the obvious economic linkage between nations—linkages that are far more binding today than in the past. 'Interdependence' has become a buzzword, and the observation that fortunes of economics move in tandem is one of the reigning platitudes of the day. Notwithstanding its repetition, the new level of interdependence remains underappreciated.

"In the past, we Americans had little cause to get excited about who was doing what to whom economically, as long as they did it on the other side of the ocean. Our economy was relatively insular. We depended on no one for resources. We produced most of what we consumed and consumed most of what we produced. When European governments crumbled under war-born economic depression, we did not feel it. While two thirds of the world wallowed in abject poverty we remained materially unaffected. The American, half a century ago, was no more affected by the economic plight of another country than he was by the crabgrass in his neighbor's lawn. As long as it didn't come under the fence, it wasn't his concern.

"Today, it is different. The crabgrass not only comes under the fence, it goes around it, climbs over it and, if left untended, will drag the fence to the ground under its weight. Today, to switch metaphors, economic problems are communicable diseases, which are highly contagious, have short incubation periods, and cannot long be quarantined."[11]

The benefits that the respondents attribute to the activities of multinational corporations are most impressive. Indeed, the scope and magnitude of these claims are such that even the most devoted adherent of multinationalism must exhibit some reservations about giving those claims his or her total endorsement. If nothing else, the statements presented so far in defense of multinational companies (as well as the words spoken in criticism) point toward the need for some method by which the performance of these organizations can be systematically assessed. However, the emotion invested in the debates by both MNC supporters and critics underscores how difficult it will be to establish assessment procedures that will command any sort of general acceptance.

Those whose comments are cited in this chapter employed a number of criteria—impact of the MNCs on living standards, the effects of these organizations on resource distribution and economic integration, their influence on international politics—to assess the performance of multinational corporations. Similarly, the one real skeptic among the respondents, Julian Bond, also referred to a number of criteria—such as concentration of economic power—as the basis for his skepticism. Perhaps the most we can hope for is that, as the debate proceeds, the participants will at least begin to see the need for agreement on some form of assessment process. Unfortunately, very little agreement exists to date on the very basic issue of defining the MNC concept, which suggests that consensus regarding the more complicated questions is many years away.

Unresolved problems

In addition to the efforts recounted thus far to define, defend, and criticize the multinational organizations, the respondents also undertook strenuous efforts to name specific difficulties that the MNCs must overcome. Among the many issues that have surfaced in response to the growth of the multinational corporation, none has caused more concern than the question of "control"—that is, the alleged need for host countries to reduce the independence that MNCs allegedly exhibit and/or the influence they exert vis-à-vis host country governments. Not all commentators agree that the MNCs enjoy an unacceptable degree of independence. Witness the remark of Felix E. Larkin, chairman of W.R. Grace & Co. "The idea of multinationals going in and taking over a country and doing as they please is largely bunk."

Similarly, Mira Wilkins (professor of economics at Florida International University), after exhaustive research on the development of multinational firms, concluded that "national sovereignties" are the dominant parties in the relationship between nations and multinational corporations. In support of her contention, she cited numerous countries with restrictions on different types of business activities, as well as some that have suffered expropriation (including Australia, Japan, the United Kingdom, Middle-East oil producing countries, and industrial Europe).[12]

Nevertheless, the concern persists that in some instances host countries must yield to the policies and preferences of the multinational firms. For example, Dr. Karl P. Sauvant, of the United Nations Centre on Transnational Corporations lists a variety of situations in which he feels greater control over MNC activities is clearly warranted.

"The most important thing that will be going on will be efforts to control transnationals, at the national level, in particular, in countries that are making an effort to do something, such as Canada, Australia, Europe, the U.S., and many developing countries. The purpose is usually threefold. One is to establish or reestablish accountability. The second one is to obtain a greater share of the benefits associated with their activities. That is particularly the case with developing countries, which frequently do not get a fair share of the benefits. And the third purpose, although less emphasized, is the question of somehow getting control over the long-term effects of transnational corporations in terms of channeling them into directions that are more favorable to self-reliant domestic growth and that might help to avoid the building of structures that are unfavorable to the developing country and to host countries in general."

The actions required to secure the control that Sauvant desires may be undertaken by individual nations or by nations acting in concert. Collective actions are most likely the best way to address a number of the other problems that the commentators have identified. For example, by any of the numerous definitions used to designate a particular company as a multinational corporation, such entities are subject to the laws and policies of more than one country. This poses a number of problems on which several of the respondents have commented. Chester Gadzinski, past president of Kearney National, is among those who have offered observations on this subject.

"Multinational corporations have already learned that they must conform to the laws of the nation in which they do business. That's a problem because working with the laws of that nation may be inconsistent with the foreign policy of the United States. This can be seen as evidenced in the oil embargo, doing business with South Africa, dealing with Rhodesia, or even doing business with Taiwan today with China looming on the horizon."

Prof. Thomas Masterson of Emory University puts the matter more succinctly, but makes the same point.

"A multinational corporation is a member of 30 or 40 different communities and its responsibility to one of those communities is by no means automatically the same as its responsibility to other communities. I see this particular problem as one of the major unresolved ones to date."

In addition to the issue of policy and legal consistency, Chester Gadzinski is concerned with the problem of tax liabilities.

"Another part of the problem is in the area of taxes and the proper allocation of corporate charges. Our Treasury Department is beginning to make noise about the fact that MNCs are understating their profits in the United States, hence, understating their tax liability."

It is certainly true that individual nations can take separate actions to alter the tax payments they receive from the MNCs operating within their boundaries. Nevertheless, international coordination on tax matters is probably a more effective way to insure that home and host countries receive predictable (and mutually satisfactory) tax payments. At the same time such consistency would help stabilize the expectations of the MNCs about what taxes are owed, when, and to which jurisdictions.

Problems that require collective action on the part of host countries were given considerable attention by former Secretary of State Dean Rusk in his comments on multinational companies.

"Every part of a multinational corporation is subject to one or another national jurisdiction. More attention should be paid to certain activities by multinationals that are not readily supervised by national authority. For example, if the multinational corporations have the capability of moving large liquid reserves rapidly from capital to capital, affecting the international monetary system and creating speculative surges here and there, that's something we might want to take a look at. If there is an unfair manipulation of prices between one country and another, that may not lend itself to strictly national jurisdiction."

Quite obviously, the actions nations can undertake individually will be far easier to accomplish than any cooperative international effort. Nations have experienced great difficulties throughout history in getting together to address far more cataclysmic problems than those posed by the multinationals. This suggests that collective action will not occur frequently, either to control undesirable behavior or to assist multinational corporations (as in bringing greater order to the legal requirements the MNCs must discharge). Yet such collective efforts must be pursued at every opportunity. In the long term, the development of consistent, truly international policies regarding the activities of multinational corporations are in the best interests of both the companies and the nations in which they operate.

Solving the MNC problem

In the previous section we considered a range of problems that restrict the performance of multinational corporations or that these same corporations create for home and host countries. For most of these problems the respondents recommended some form of remedial action, although specific solutions were not discussed in great detail. More concrete proposals have been made for addressing the problems associated with multinational business organizations. These range from recommendations for action by a single individual to activities that are as multinational in scope as the organizations on which they focus.

The image problem

Among the many difficulties multinational corporations currently face is the rash of bad publicity that has emerged in recent years. A number of factors can be cited to account for the development of this problem. They include revelations about the involvement of MNC officials in bribery and political corruption, the alleged insensitivity of multinationals to social conditions in underdeveloped countries, and the general cynicism with which the public views many of our large modern institutions. In the view of one respondent, Arthur R. Taylor, former president of the Columbia Broadcasting System, this major image problem could be remedied through the efforts of one person.

"This adverse publicity cannot be effectively

countered until some well-known person for whom the public has great respect comes forward to plead the cause of the multinationals. I think that the case for the multinational is very persuasive. Why isn't it understood? There have clearly been many booklets and talks on the subject. It's because the case is not being put forward by a figure who has the public's sympathy and creditability. If Dwight Eisenhower were alive and would support the multinational corporations, do you think most Americans would believe him? Of course they would! But that's our problem. The American business community does not have the kind of articulate, charismatic, passionately devoted leadership it needs to give a very good case a chance of succeeding."

Although the public esteem of business leaders has dropped in recent years, the business community has a good chance to recover much of this lost prestige. To do so it must show itself capable of helping to solve important problems about which the public is concerned. In a similar vein, the best hope the multinational firms have for gaining public confidence (in the United States and elsewhere) is through effectively helping to resolve various social problems. This will continue to be a tiresome and thankless task, especially since the needs and desires of the publics whom the MNCs affect are so diverse. Nevertheless, a strategy of this sort is more promising than waiting for and depending on a proponent of multinational enterprise who approaches Eisenhower-like credibility. The appearance of such an individual on the current scene is not likely. Moreover, even if a person of the sort Taylor envisions did appear, the effect on public attitudes would not be as positive or as long-lasting as the impact of the problem-solving approach.

Bringing MNCs and governments together

The necessity for exerting greater control over the activities of multinational corporations within individual nations is a problem that has been already alluded to. Former U.N. Ambassador Andrew Young suggests that, in order to deal with this problem, multinational corporations must be more explicitly integrated into the political process.

"Right now the State Department is dealing with foreign policy, the Treasury Department is dealing with monetary policy and trade policy, and the Commerce Department is giving advice about investments, and the three aren't talking to each other within the government—at least that was the case in the past three administrations. So any sensible foreign policy is going to have to involve the Departments of State, Treasury, and Commerce. But it is also going to have to involve a relationship with the multinational corporations.

"Normally, the multinational corporations are accused of influencing politics and we tend to want to keep them separate. I don't believe in that. I think that you can bring them together and cooperate if it is done in the open. It is ridiculous to say that corporations don't influence politics. They influence it negatively most of the time because they do it by reacting to circumstances rather than by thinking through matters in advance and by having access to the kinds of political intelligence that they need to do business.

"There is a model in Japan. The top 25 corporations in Japan meet periodically with the government to discuss the national interests. This puts the corporations, the public sector, and the government in a much better light.

"In Africa or Eastern Europe, U.S. investment policy could do a lot more than the CIA to determine the development process. We all have a basic self-interest in orderly progress throughout the world. And we are not going to be able to do that without talking to each other. I am not talking about government planning for business. But I am talking about periodic conversations between government and business."

Naturally, a proposal to involve elements of the business community more closely in the formulation of the national government's business and foreign policies raises serious questions. First, there is the matter of who participates. Great selectivity would have to be exercised to insure that only those business leaders who could contribute substantively to the policy formulation effort and who could also assist in implementing the policy thus developed were invited to take part. Also, there would be many more aspirants than space available. Some effort would be needed to assuage the feelings of those who were not selected, since many of these people may feel disappointed and aggrieved.

Second, policy formulation would have to be conducted in such a way that none of the business participants could secure "inside" information that would give them an advantage over competitors.[13] Perhaps the most effective way to avoid problems in this area is to insure that all deliberations are open to the public and the mass media.

Despite the possible difficulties associated with Young's proposal, the regular contact and consultation could offer many additional opportunities to develop a more integrated national policy in the fields of international business and foreign affairs. The term *integrated national policy* is, of course, extremely vague. Basically, it refers to an overall policy in which the economic and foreign affairs programs of the national government are not in conflict, and it is hoped are even in harmony, with the activities of foreign private business organizations. The concept would surely include companies based within the national government's jurisdiction. Conceivably, the concept could be expanded to include foreign-based firms operating in areas in which the national government has foreign policy interests of high priority.

The advantages that would accrue from the development and maintenance of such an integrated policy suggest that the risks associated with Young's suggestion are definitely warranted. In pursuit of these coordinated policy objectives. multinational corporations might, for example, be persuaded to invest in areas in which the State Department wanted to promote economic development. By the same token, business participants might use the discussions to alert government policymakers to plan to establish new manufacturing operations or marketing efforts outside the United States. Government participants could possibly offer useful insights about the successful conduct of these operations.

International efforts concerning multinationals

The proposals that Young offers relate primarily to situations in which a single government may wish to better coordinate or control one or more multinational corporations. There are, however, other instances in which a number of governments must be involved in resolving issues that arise from MNC operations. The respondents made several suggestions that bear on situations of this type. The recommendations range from general recommendations to very specific proposals. Generally, harmony and the spirit of compromise should form the resolution of burning issues involving multinational firms and sovereign governments. More specifically, international machinery should be used both to establish standards of conduct for multinational corporations and to monitor adherence to those standards.

Recommendations concerning harmony and compromise come from Thornton Bradshaw, chairman of the board of RCA. His basic contention is that a rough sort of comity should characterize the relationship among multinational firms, home governments, and host governments. All these parties must recognize, Bradshaw argues, that each has valid claims to make on the others. A spirit of accommodation and partnership should make it possible for each party's claims to be received and realized to some extent. Having voiced these uplifting sentiments, however, Bradshaw acknowledged his very real doubts that anything like the cooperative spirit he advocates will emerge in the forseeable future. The rising spirit of nationalism, he fears, will preclude the realization of his hopes.

Tightening the hold on MNCs

In contrast to Bradshaw's proposals are those of William Winpisinger, president of the International Association of Machinists, who advocates exerting greater control over multinational firms. He focuses less on cooperation and more on adversarial relationships. In Winpisinger's view, the resolution of issues concerning multinational corporations will have a profound impact on future economic trends. "We have a problem with the multinationals, and what labor can do in terms of coming to grip with this problem, on a broader or transnational basis, will determine to some extent what will happen in the 1980s and 1990s."

The specific problems Winpisinger has identified concerning multinational firms include capital outflow from the United States and the tax advantages MNCs now enjoy. Winpisinger suggests two basic strategies for dealing with these issues.

"It has to be one of two ways. Either we will have to come to grips with it legislatively in our own country or come to grips with it in combination with the balance of the free world trade unions on a transnational or multinational basis. We need some kind of a bargaining mechanism that would go beyond national boundaries just as profit-making enterprises do. I view the former to be much more easily accomplished than the latter. But if we must go the hard way we will have to tackle it on the latter basis. It will take a little longer, but there is no doubt that we can put it together. All that it requires is sufficient aggravation.

"It would be preferable to see some comprehensive legislation right here in our own country.

There are all kinds of suggestions. I don't know which would be the most effective, but certainly, dollar for dollar, tax write-offs don't do much to stop it or discourage it. Untaxed profits, unless they come back to the United States, aren't much of a deterent. I hear American businessmen constantly lamenting the present stature of the economy as it relates to capital formation in the future. I'm not terribly impressed with that when I am aware that 25 cents of every dollar invested last year alone went into overseas investments.

"If we have to worry about capital formation at home, maybe what we should do is keep it at home. Maybe we should not let money go abroad where it creates untaxed profits, which do the American people no good. As often as not, current policies provide multinationals with a dollar-for-dollar tax write-off. The American people become worse off because there is that much less for the federal treasury."

It is conceivable that, in the course of some future "tax reform" effort, the U.S. Congress could enact legislation that overturns the tax benefits multinational corporations now enjoy and about which Winpisinger is concerned. The prospects for congressional curtailment of overseas capital investments are more uncertain. Business spokespersons can and do offer persuasive arguments about the need for such investment practices. For example, investment in a particular country may be perceived as a prerequisite to an effective sales effort there. Often a foreign nation will not buy a company's product unless the company builds a plant. In the United States that would be looked upon as blackmail, but often in the foreign market it's not. This is, of course, a rather extreme perception of the link between investment and sales patterns. However, this same linkage has been noted by Donald Kendall, who expressed the point in a more restrained fashion.

"MNC officials learned that if they wanted to hold onto or even enter into certain markets, they had only one choice: produce where they were going to sell. Despite theories to the contrary, the evidence is compelling that the choice for most American companies has rarely been investing in foreign operations, but rather between investing in foreign operations or losing out to a competitor.

"A research team commissioned by the U.S. Department of Commerce made an in-depth study of U.S.–foreign direct investment. The team concluded that, in most cases, U.S. firms do not have the alternative of continuing to serve the relevant market—either in the United States or abroad—from their U.S. plants. If these firms tried to continue operating only in the United States, they would lose their markets to foreign firms, usually to large enterprises from Europe and Japan."

Tax benefits are more susceptible to action by Congress because these advantages can be classified as "loopholes." As such, they have a certain vulnerability any time tax reform proposals come under congressional consideration.

What of Winpisinger's suggestion that the international trade union community can be an effective instrument in changing the behavior of the multinational corporations? It is possible that a coalition of these groups could, through an international bargaining effort, alter the investment practices or strategies of multinational firms to repatriate profits. However, securing agreement among the coalition members on issues that affect vital national interests will be extremely difficult, even under the most favorable circumstances. Such difficulties will be doubly evident with particular questions, such as investment practices, which obviously affect job distribution. Perhaps, however, the "bottom line" to Winpisinger's recommendation is that an international coalition of trade unionists would, by definition, be unable to pursue a narrow set of economic interests vis-à-vis the multinationals. Such a coalition would have to adopt a program designed to foster a broad range of interests. Nevertheless, the obstacles to developing such a program would be immense.

The interest Winpisinger expresses in international efforts to influence the behavior of multinational corporations is even more strongly advanced by former Secretary of State Henry A. Kissinger. International organizations, Kissinger believes, offer a vital mechanism for dealing with MNCs and the issues these organizations engender.

> The United States . . . believes that the time has come for the international community to articulate standards of conduct for both enterprises and governments. The United Nations Commission on Transnational Corporations, and other international bodies, have begun such an effort. We must reach agreement on balanced principles. These should apply to transnational enterprises in their relations with governments, and to governments in their relations with enterprises and with other governments. They must be fair principles, for failure to reflect the interests of all parties concerned would exacerbate rather than moderate the frictions which have damaged the environments for international investment.[14]

In another instance, Dr. Kissinger acknowledged that a formal treaty that would formulate "binding rules for multinational enterprises does not seem possible in the near future."[15] Nevertheless, the United States is committed to working with other countries to establish a code of conduct that provides guidance and direction for multinational corporations.

> The United States believes an agreed statement of basic principles is achievable. We are prepared to make a major effort and invite the participation of all interested parties. We support the relevant work of the UN Commission on Transnational Enterprises. We believe that such guidelines must:
>
> > Accord with existing principles of international law governing the treatment of foreigners and their property rights.
> >
> > Call upon multinational corporations to take account of national priorities, act in accordance with local law, and employ fair labor practices.
> >
> > Cover all multinationals, state-owned as well as private.

Not discriminate in favor of host country enterprises except under specifically defined and limited circumstances.

Set forth not only the obligations of the multinationals, but also the host country's responsibilities to the foreign enterprises within their borders.

Acknowledge the responsibility of governments to apply recognized conflict-of-laws principles in reconciling regulations applied by various host nations.

If multinational institutions become an object of economic warfare, it will be an ill omen for the global economic system. We believe that the continued operation of transnational companies, under accepted guidelines, can be reconciled with the claims of national sovereignty. The capacity of nations to deal with this issue constructively will be a test of whether the search for common solutions or the clash of ideologies will dominate our economic future."[16]

Kissinger's commitment to working within the context of international organizations is not limited to the United Nations. He also sees the Organization for Economic Cooperation and Development as having an important role in this connection. Kissinger feels that it is "highly significant [that OECD] undertook two related tasks: to negotiate voluntary guidelines for multinational firms and to clarify governmental responsibilities to preserve and promote a liberal investment climate."[17] In addition to the UN and OECD, Kissinger has also identified a role for the World Bank in helping settle disputes arising out of the investments efforts. "Fact-finding and arbitral procedures must be promoted as means for settling investment disputes. The World Bank's International Center for the Settlement of Investment Disputes, and other third-party facilities, should be employed to settle the important disputes which inevitably arise."[18]

To complement these activities on the part of various supranational bodies, Kissinger urges nations to work out bilateral and multilateral arrangements. These arrangements would deal with mechanisms for handling problems associated with multinational corporations.

> "Governments must harmonize their tax treatment of these enterprises. Without coordination, host-country and home-country policies may inhibit productive investments. Laws against restrictive business practices must be developed, better coordinated among countries, and enforced. The United States has long been vigilant against such abuses in domestic trade, mergers, or licensing of technology. We stand by the same principles internationally. We condemn restrictive practices in setting prices or restraining supplies, whether by private or state-owned transnational enterprises or by the collusion of national governments. Insurance for foreign private investors should to the extent possible be multilateralized, and should include financial participation by developing countries to reflect our mutual stake in encouraging foreign investment in the service of development. And there must be more effective bilateral consultation among governments to identify and resolve investment disputes before they become irritants in political relations."[19]

The limits of proposals to date

In view of the difficulties of getting nations to agree on common courses of action, how likely is it that even the voluntary guidelines and codes of conduct that Kissinger supports will be effective?[20] In terms of securing the desired compliance on the part of multinational corporations, the voluntary guidelines have very definite limitations. The guidelines are important, however, because they represent a beginning, however incomplete and faulty. They are a first step toward a clearer definition of the behavior expected of multinational firms. At present, the expectations entertained by MNC managers, governments, consumers, suppliers, and employees are as diverse and abundant as the various definitions of *multinational corpo-*

ration. The efforts by the United Nations and the OECD may be the first steps in developing a consensus shared by the MNCs and their various constituents as to the obligations each party must discharge in relation to the others. A perfect consensus, of course, cannot be anticipated. The world is filled with limitations, contingencies, and human sin. Even an imperfect but workable agreement is years away. At present, the best that can be hoped for is that initial efforts, such as those referred to by Henry A. Kissinger, can be continued and, when possible, expanded.

MNCs in the 80s and 90s

What can multinational corporations expect in the 1980s and 1990s? The views expressed by the interviewees range from a prognosis of "more of the same" to projections of qualitative change in the way multinational corporations operate. For his part, Arthur R. Taylor foresees little change except, perhaps, in the attitudes of host countries. Taylor does not, however, expect these attitudinal changes to have a serious impact on MNC activities. "I don't see MNCs expanding their horizons and I don't see the host countries becoming anything except more quarrelsome. I don't see any fundamental changes in the way in which the multinationals operate."

On the other hand, Felix Larkin feels that host country attitudes will moderate. However, because of the previous hostilities multinational corporations have encountered, Larkin envisions them exhibiting increased wariness in dealing with their hosts.

"One interesting aspect regarding multinationals, which is starting already, is the complete reversal of attitude by most of the host countries. They are now getting terrified that the multinationals are going to pull out. Many of the multinationals are pulling out or reducing because they find that the atmosphere is hostile or difficult to financially survive. And so, the multinational's role will be a combination of the hospitality of the host countries and a more cautious attitude on the part of the multinationals."

Despite the conflicting views these commentators express about host country attitudes, their basic conclusions are quite similar. Thornton Bradshaw, however, forecasts substantial changes for the multinationals, at least for those in the petroleum industry.

"The multinationals are going to be buffeted a good deal. The oil industry, for instance, will probably not be a multinational by the middle 1980s. It certainly will not be a multinational in terms of holding reserves around the world. It may be a contractor to various governments around the world, but it will obviously not have the decision-making power in terms of whether to produce or not to produce, whether to explore or not to explore, whom to deliver the oil to, etc. It will not have the kind of decision-making power that it had in the past. In actuality, it does not have that kind of power today. And this has been an extraordinarily large change."

Given the continuing assertiveness on the part of the oil-producing nations with respect to prices and ownership of production facilities, it is difficult to argue with Bradshaw's overall assessment: "Is the multinational here to stay? Will it be able to change in the way it is set up now? You see more and more companies that have gone into Brazil, Argentina, and Europe being nationalized. They go in and develop to a point where they become profitable, where they have added to the country, raised the standard of living. Then the government comes in and takes them over. You also see more and more companies in Europe being run by foreign nationals. You see more and more worker participation on the boards of directors of these companies. The whole complexion of multinationals is going to change. As long as we keep in mind that we've got the capital, the wealth, and the technology, we can strike a balance. The multinationals are not going to be the profit makers they once were. The Union Carbides, DuPonts, and IBMs are not going to be able to take profits out of those countries like they have in the past. We need to export American technology. There is a definite role for the multinational in the future—maybe, not as profitable."

Finally, Dr. Donald P. Jacobs, dean of the graduate school of management at Northwestern University, predicts the entry of a large number of new multinational firms in the world business arena. These firms will most likely represent areas from which MNCs have not previously emerged.

"Multinational companies will continue to grow as they have in the postwar period. The major development will be the vast number of new companies that will become multinational in their operations. Prior to World War II, the field of multinational activities was not dominated by American companies. A number of European and American companies, as well as some Japanese trading companies, engaged in multinational activities. In the first two decades after World War II, this multinational development was dominated largely by American companies. It was only in the last decade that European and Japanese companies came into their own. The interesting aspect will be the entrance into the multinational field by companies domiciled in Europe, South America, Asia, South Africa, and possibly the Middle East, as well as additional American companies. I believe this will be a desirable development, since one of the major concerns underlying the criticism of multinational development has been the large scale of dominance by American companies."

Although it would be extremely imprudent to characterize the comments in this chapter as reflecting any sort of broad consensus, there are a number of common threads that are evident in the different contributions the respondents have offered.

First, the multinational corporation has an enviable life expectancy. The MNC is certainly not a new phenomenon; nevertheless, it will continue to participate in world economic affairs long after all of us have lost interest. Its projected longevity is more than enough to dishearten its critics and detractors. It might be well to recall that the late President Eisenhower warned against a return to what he called an inept, selfish, and self-defeating system of economic nationalism. This warning must be renewed today. The attack on the multinational company could easily lead to such a system. The multinational company must be treated for what it is—a modern and flexible means for providing the goods and services people need, both in America and all over the world.

Notwithstanding these observations, the environment in which the multinational corporation operates will change appreciably over the next decade. As Thornton Bradshaw pointed out, the oil-producing countries will certainly demand (and secure) a more decisive role in the management of the multinationals that operate within their boundaries. The changes that the multinationals other than oil companies must accommodate may not be as drastic as those that the oil companies will confront. But there are likely to be increased demands for a greater distribution of the benefits derived from most MNC operations to host country governments, if not their residents.

Third, the transnational efforts to set standards and guidelines for multinational behavior will not abate. Nor will they coalesce around any comprehensive consensus about how MNCs ought to operate. As indicated earlier, these efforts ought to be encouraged, but no one should harbor much hope that they will result in a uniform set of standards around which MNC managers and directors can focus company policy, plans, and activities.

Finally, as Donald Kendall has suggested, the most significant difference between the present and the past is the increased interest in multinational corporations and their activities. "What is new about multinational corporations is that in the past few years they suddenly seem to have come under sharp scrutiny by international organizations, government agencies, university centers, business associations, trade unions, and many individuals." The intense scrutiny to which Kendall refers will certainly continue. In fact, it will more likely increase in the coming decade.

4

Productivity and the new work force

One of the most profound demographic developments of the 1960s and the 1970s was the sharp decrease in the nation's birthrate. A dramatic increase in the birthrate after World War II produced the much discussed baby boom of the late 1940s and 1950s. During that period the number of children born to the average woman in her lifetime reached 3.8, almost twice the replacement rate of 2.1. (The "replacement rate" is the number of children each woman must bear if the population is to remain stable.) At the time this book goes to press, the fertility rate will be down to 1.76, well below the replacement rate level.[1]

The *Business Week* article that reported this data also speculated on the impact that changing birthrates will have on the makeup of the work force in the 1980s. The article anticipates that the baby boom generation will continue to exert considerable pressure on the job market, at least through the first half of this decade.[2] For the near future, therefore, competition among baby boomers for desirable entry-level jobs will be vigorous indeed. Moreover, as those people grow older, the competition will continue although the stakes will change. The large number of candidates will mean many of those aspiring to senior management and professional positions cannot be accommodated.

In addition, the large baby boom cohort will offer unique challenges to other work-force members. In the short term, there will be an unusually large number of junior managers and professionals in proportion to those in the more senior brackets. This situation will pose unique supervision problems for executive management. Their tasks will be made no less difficult by the frustration and resentment the younger person may feel because of reduced advancement opportunities.[3]

The impact of this large cohort of younger workers is not, of course, the only personnel challenge that must be addressed by management in the 1980s. For the last 15 to 20 years we have witnessed a great upsurge in protest by past victims of employment discrimination, most notably minority group members and women. The demands these groups have voiced for improved job opportunities are not likely to abate in the next decade. Indeed, if State Senator Julian Bond of Georgia is correct, such pressures will not only continue to be forceful but will also be more skillfully applied in the next decade. (See Bond's comments in Chapter 2.) Senior managers will continue to face challenges to traditional personnel practices that will require substantive changes in the way companies have customarily hired, promoted, fired, and retired their personnel. Of course, many companies have already made drastic adjustments in personnel policies. Nevertheless, many more adjustments by many more companies will be necessary in the next 10 years. All sectors of business had best prepare for these additional challenges.

In offering their projections and recommendations concerning personnel issues, the respondents addressed a number of specific topics. Areas of discussion included the changing nature of the

personnel function within the corporations, requirements and strategies for increasing opportunities for women and minorities, and alternative
proposals for increasing productivity.

The emerging corporate personnel office

Quite often in the past, the personnel function
has been a dumping ground for nonproductive
members of management circles. It has been a
paper-shuffling activity that could only attract the
attention and appreciation of top management by
recommending benefit changes contrary to corporate philosophy (which personnel usually had no
part in determining) or by pulling on the chains
that held it captive within lower-middle management ranks.

Today the personnel function is undergoing a
complete face-lift. Personnel professionals must
have the knowledge to deal with the changing
work force and statutory requirements. They must
be familiar with sophisticated analytical methods
of planning and evaluation. They must have sufficient knowledge of the organization and management to diagnose organizational problems and develop imaginative and pragmatic solutions to
those problems impartially. Finally, the personnel
professional must be sensitive to problems of
ethics and competing values.

Law, regulation, and public opinion are forcing
corporate personnel officers to create greater opportunity for women and minorities and to improve work life conditions, among other responsibilities. Personnel administrators who are
merely paper shufflers are increasingly being replaced by those with qualifications equal to the
task.

The personnel function is emerging as a function of unprecedented importance. The scope of
its responsibilities has expanded into practically
every aspect of a company's activity. The manner
in which those responsibilities are discharged has
never been more crucial to a company's success.

The social, economic, and legal atmosphere in which business operates today makes it imperative to include the personnel function in primary planning and development at the top management level and to hold the personnel function accountable on a profit-and-loss basis.

In recent years, American workers in large numbers have embraced a bewildering array of new values and interests. Moreover, today's employees are not only cognizant of their civil rights; they boldly demand that these rights be respected. The level of competence and professional accomplishment is high among executive managers in many business organizations. However, their training and experiences have not prepared them in all cases to integrate corporate goals with programs designed to address the real interests that employees express for improving the quality of work life.

Clearly the personnel problems of today and tomorrow demand expertise and specialization. The personnel area is too crucial and errors are too costly to permit haphazard handling of these problems. Line managers, heretofore fairly autonomous where their employees were concerned, must relinquish much of this independence to insure competent consolidation of the company's personnel policies. Centralization is a word that causes great fear among many management personnel, but standardization of policy is a must where the law requires equality and employees demand fairness. Obviously, every department manager in an organizational structure cannot proceed independently where fair and uniform treatment is involved.

There can be little doubt that personnel officers must take the lead in executing the corporate philosophy related to its treatment of employees. But doubt exists in many cases whether the personnel staff can do that adequately. Habitually relegated to a second-class status in the structure of the organization, personnel departments now find themselves short of the training and experience needed. The expertise required to interpret the implications of new laws and trends for the whole company simply exceeds the capabilities of many personnel professionals. The suddenness, magnitude, and complexity of new developments have left many personnel administrators baffled and bewildered. Often problems are swept under the rug and hasty, shortsighted solutions formulated.

In assessing the role of the modern personnel professional, we immediately confront a critical dilemma. There is, on the one hand, an obvious and pressing need that such professionals contribute substantively to the formulation of their organizations' basic business plans and policies. Yet the skills and insights that personnel officials need for this vital task are in noticeably short supply.

This dilemma is examined critically in the comments of one of the respondents, Prof. Fred K. Foulkes of Boston University.

"The personnel function is becoming increasingly important because top management recognizes that it can make substantial contributions to the business. In addition, if the personnel staff don't act well, many problems can come about that are extremely expensive, be they class action suits with respect to equal opportunity employment or risks of plant shutdowns or inspections because of safety and health problems."

The great opportunities that await the skillful and aggressive personnel professional have not escaped the notice of Prof. Thomas R. Masterson of Emory University. Masterson foresees tremendous increases in the responsibility potentially available to a person now called a human resource director; if he or she is competent enough, can see far into the future, and is willing to work for important goals, then he or she has an area of corporate responsibility that can be carved out with literally no boundaries. In Masterson's view, human resources are far more important than monetary assets.

"It is a truism that the human resources of any organization are the most valuable asset that an institution possesses. When we try to do human resource accounting we find that we are not able to put people onto a balance sheet in a strictly monetary sense. But we will be able to determine which of our people are most developable, where we have young people coming from and into, and who has the potential for vast individual development."

The awesome array of personnel issues and problems that are converging on contemporary business organizations account for the increasing importance of the personnel officer. Strictly speaking, of course, the personnel function has always been a significant activity, or at least it should have been treated as such. Certainly the failure on the part of many businesses to take personnel activities seriously is one reason so many pressing difficulties have accumulated for today's managers. As already indicated, the very legitimate demands for increased employment opportunity voiced by women and members of minority groups are among the chief issues personnel officials must address. A number of the respondents have commented on this particular issue.

Changing roles of women and minorities in business

There are many reasons managers, corporate officers, and directors of American business organizations should endorse and support programs for increasing employment opportunities for minorities and women. The moral imperative to assist victims of discrimination and prejudice is certainly the most compelling consideration. There has never been, and there will never be, any valid reason for denying employment opportunities to individuals simply because they happen to be black, Hispanic, Oriental, or Native Americans. Neither has there ever been a conceivable reason for discriminating against people because of their gender. These ethical concerns ought to be the prime motivation for modern managers to initiate and maintain aggressive efforts to redress the wrongs that minority group members and women have suffered because of employment discrimination.

Moreover, after the case for employment opportunities for minority group members and women has been thoroughly justified on moral grounds, there remains the practical advantages that can accrue to individual companies and to American business generally where such employment opportunities are expanded. Former U.N. Ambassador Andrew Young feels that the effectiveness of U.S. enterprise in readying overseas markets can be improved through increased employment opportunities for minorities.

"This will be good business, especially in terms of the color differences, because American business is going to make more profit when it is racially sensitive abroad. For example, if Nigeria has $80 billion out of their oil revenues that they intend to spend in the 1980s for development, companies that go over there with integrated bidding teams are going to get the contracts. It is simply because Nigerians are very race conscious. They aren't racists but they are going to be very sensitive about any lily-white operation coming over there."

In a similar vein, Young argues persuasively that, with the scarcity of trained people in many fields, it is foolish to forgo using the talents and skills of any competent individual. Concerning the benefits associated with increased work opportunities for women, former Commerce Secretary Juanita Kreps observes that improving job prospects for female workers can also help men.

"If we believe that women's job expectations will continue to rise as in recent years, it will surely follow that a wider range of work- and life-styles will have to be available to both sexes. Traditionally male jobs will have to be filled by women in increasing numbers. And more options, including more free time, will be opened to men."

How are we to overcome the barriers to greater business career involvement faced by minorities and women? According to Sally Levy of the Orleans Transportation Service, basic attitudinal changes on the part of senior managers are vitally needed.

"We still have a long way to go despite the fact that the opportunities are there. The basic problem today, which will of course continue into the future, is that despite the opportunities we are still living in a very male chauvinistic society. The attitudes of men in business toward women are not only directed from the management level. There are more and more women and minority members graduating from college. More women are not going directly into marriage and are seeking careers. They are taking courses in college that were really not open to women five or ten years ago, such as architecture and engineering. However, it is the attitude of big business that women come in at a lower level or on a lower pay scale than men. These women have the same qualifications and college degrees as the men. It is business, as a general rule, that expects more of women than of male counterparts. The women are scrutinized more thoroughly, their work processes are checked more thoroughly, their performance evaluations are placed at a higher level. In order for women in the next five or ten years to reach the peaks of success that they feel themselves capable of reaching, the attitudes within management are going to have to change."

Interestingly, Levy believes that negative attitudes about recruitment and promotion of women are rapidly giving way at the lower organizational levels, where hiring decisions are often made. Thus, despite the opposition of senior managers, who Levy labels "the old guard," increased employment opportunities for women are emerging in today's business world. Even greater progress could be forthcoming, of course, if the old guard views were also changed.

To some, Levy's contention—that attitudes at the lower corporate levels are basically sympathetic to equal employment opportunities for women and minority groups—will seem unduly optimistic, if not downright naive. Nevertheless, at least one other respondent, Juanita Kreps, shares some of Levy's view. Kreps argues that the basic issue today is improving overall corporate performance. Questions about the basic competence of women and minority group members have been satisfactorily resolved, she asserts. The key concern must now be overcoming the many deficiencies that are evident in the way business organizations generally conduct their operations.

"Surely, we no longer need to document intellectual capacities or the willingness to take on the tough jobs, nor does any corporation need further evidence that performance on these jobs is not sex-related. Harping on ability is not going to speed progress and it may hurt. Instead of looking for on-the-job differences between men and women, we should be looking for deficiencies in performance irrespective of sex, age, or race, and asking what could be done to correct those deficiencies. Instead of asking whether women will make better or worse decisions on boards, we should be seeking ways to improve the flow of information to the directors to enable them to come to wiser conclusions. Instead of asking whether women directors will concern themselves with consumer or affirmative action issues, we should constantly pose that all-important question: What are the corporation's responsibilities in these areas? Whether such farsightedness more often resides in men or women is not the issue. Rather, we must ask how to improve corporate decisions by directing the board's attention to important new areas of social policy."

In addition to these general perspectives on the employment outlook for women and minorities, the respondents offered some specific suggestions about how to expand further the employment opportunities available to women. Dr. Anne Harlan of Wellesley College believes that the presence of an influential role model may help account for the success enjoyed by the relatively small number of women who have risen to senior management positions. Other types of assistance are required, Harlan argues, when role models are not available. Her research on the emerging role of women in the workplace is exhaustive and comprehensive.

"I believe women now are able to enter nontraditional jobs such as management fairly easily, but the real dilemma is advancing within those jobs. For years, companies have assumed that women entering management were different from men in similar positions and required special training to correct their deficiencies. Thus, women were asked to attend many programs designed exclusively for women and ranging from assertiveness training to math anxiety. Based on the work conducted by Dr. Carol Weiss and me, these assumptions appear to be faulty.

"In our recent study of over 200 managers, we were struck by the similarities between men and women. The sexes were indistinguishable on the bases of psychological characteristics or skill level. The difficulties experienced in their careers were quite similar except that women faced the additional pressure of sex bias, sometimes overt, sometimes subtle. To have placed these women in special programs designed to help them succeed not only highlights career differences between men and women that appear to be more imagined than real, but also overlooks the needs of men holding similar positions.

"Special programs designed to help women may also contribute to the emergence of sex bias as they are usually seen in one of two ways. First, other organizational members could view women as deficient in important skills, reinforcing the idea of women being less capable than men. Second, women could be seen as receiving 'favored' treatment, reinforcing feelings of injustice and reverse discrimination. Both of these views would increase the alienation and tension between men and women managers in the organization.

"If programs designed exclusively for women are not the answer, what then can organizations do to further women's probability of success? For the answer to this question, I return to what I see as the two biggest barriers facing women in organizations. One of these barriers men share; the other is unique to women: (1) gaining additional skills needed for advancement; and (2) overcoming sex bias.

"In our work, Dr. Weiss and I found that both men and women managers often failed to advance because of personal deficiencies in managerial skills needed at the next level of management. The most common skill areas needing improvement were delegating of work, long-term planning, employee development, and career management.

"We feel organizations should develop more comprehensive training programs that focus on skill acquisition and improvement. Efforts should be made to include both men and women in such programs. Working together will reinforce their similarity as well as provide an opportunity for them to interact as equals.

"Dealing with sex bias is more difficult. I now believe eradicating sex bias from organizations is not possible. Therefore, organizational policies must be aimed at controlling the potentially harmful effects of sex bias. Policy areas that should be examined in detail include recruitment, selection and promotion policies, and corporate reward policies.

"Job promotions and increased opportunity for growth and challenge are highly valued by both male and female managers. Sex bias seems to emerge, in part, as a result of competition for advancement opportunity. In the absence of sufficient information about available jobs and selection criteria, both men and women may overestimate the 'competitive edge' the other sex has. Men assume women have a greater likelihood of attaining highly desirable positions because of affirmative action pressures; women assume men are more apt to attain such positions because of the operation of an 'old boy network' and bias against women.

"Two steps are important to decrease the tension likely to result from promotion decisions. First of all, information about job opportunities must be made available to all interested, qualified persons, regardless of sex. One of the most efficient means of conveying this information is through a job posting system. Secondly, valid criteria for selection should be identified and used in making the selection.

"The first step in determining valid criteria should be the identification of competencies needed for successful job performance. This competency assessment would then form the base for job descriptions, selection procedures, and evaluation criteria. Selection criteria must change as needed competencies for job performance change. Thus, follow-up at future points in time would be essential to determine needed competencies. This procedure not only makes the selection process easier and more likely to produce a better job-person fit. It is also especially helpful for men and women desiring to assess realistically their own performance and development needs. Care must be taken, however, to identify and use criteria that are not subtly biased in favor of one sex. Educational credentials, for example, are widely used by most organizations as a selection criterion for higher-level jobs. However, this criterion has a typically low validity in predicting future job performance and a high likelihood of operating against the selection of women and minorities.

"Similarly, organizations should examine their reward policies carefully. Managers should be held accountable and rewarded for the training and development of employees reporting to them, both male and female. In this way, women will have greater access to the informal training that is often so important to later success.

"The outcome of these efforts, I believe, will be good human resource management as well as greater opportunity for women. By clearly identifying competencies needed for job performance, selecting valid criteria and using those criteria in hiring and promotion decisions, much of the bias inherent in less formal selection procedures will disappear. Likewise, implementing strategies that ensure training and development for all employees is good management practice, which will encourage better utilization of women as well as men."

Thomas H. Paine of Hewitt Associates (a management consulting group specializing in employee benefits and compensation) predicts that the 1980s and 1990s will witness the greater acceptance of "partial careers;" that is, either second careers or careers interrupted by childbirth. This concept can conceivably be adopted by individual firms but will require far greater modification of current organizational practice than would the adoption of Harlan's recommendations.

"We discriminate terribly against women and minorities by arranging the best rewards to go to the ones that work at the same place for 30 years. The promotional system and pyramidal structure of most organizations enhances that. For example, in a company such as AT&T, women can't be vice presidents of such and such because they didn't work their way up through the system, and because they can't work their way up through the system that fast. When a woman drops out of the labor force to have a baby and raise her family, she drops out of that reward system. When she comes back, she begins at the bottom. We are going to see ourselves having more acceptance of the multiple career, and women will be a major beneficiary of it. Many men will also be beneficiaries because right now it is not very acceptable to be unemployed when you are 45."

Frances Knight Palmeri, editor and publisher of "Women's Work," a national journal on career planning, is optimistic though patient.

"Even though there are tremendous and often seemingly insurmountable barriers to further progress by women, the trends that we see will not be arrested but will probably be accelerated. True integration by gender may be decades away, but the 1980s will be a time when we can at least look at trends to see what progress is being made in the white-collar as well as the blue-collar areas. Women must understand that there is a 'getting your head together' requirement that cuts across all age and occupation groups.

"It's important that women have appropriate role models to follow. The first women in, say, the lower upper levels of a corporation, the first women on a board of directors, the first women president of even a middle-sized corporation, will be excellent role models for women to follow. The so-called trail blazers will make it easier for other women. So role models are very important."

In summary, then, the commentators feel that unusual job opportunities for women and minority group members (people who have been victims of employment discrimination for generations) will benefit both those whose employment prospects are increased and the businesses that increase career opportunities. Moreover, two of the commentators have argued that increased employment opportunities for women will have a beneficial impact on male workers as well. How likely is it that increased employment opportunities for women and members of minority groups will actually materialize in the next decade? Thomas Paine, who expresses confidence that the "partial career" concept will enjoy greater acceptance in the coming years, offers this cautiously optimistic forecast.

"Most institutions have a major commitment to recognize discrimination against women and minorities and to do something about it. The distribution of women in work places will be, without a doubt, very different from what it is today. We are going to most likely give women and minorities an equal opportunity to get a job in the future. Generally, we legally pay men and women the same for the same job, but the cries from minorities and women suggest that we may in fact not be. This was the original thrust of the EEOC [Equal Employment Opportunity Commission]. What has to be done is to assure ourselves that minorities and women have the equal opportunity of getting that better job."

Georgia state senator Julian Bond seems less optimistic. He forsees less voluntary effort on the part of businesses to insure that women and minority group members are given adequate employment opportunity. "I have a fear that the minority groups in this country, both blacks and women (who are actually the majority but treated like a minority), are not going to get their just due from the American corporate structure without first increasing government controls and some form of pressure."

I, personally, greatly respect the insight and perception that Bond usually brings to his assessments of social and political issues. In this particular instance, however, I unreservedly hope that Bond's prediction is wrong. I hope instead that my colleagues and associates in the business community will give full support to all legitimate efforts to expand the employment and career prospects of women and members of minority groups.

The materials and observations surveyed thus far suggest that the U. S. work force will undergo several significant changes between now and the end of the 1980s. All members of the work force will be required to adapt to numerous new situations and challenges. Managers will face the task of incorporating people into the work force (and into promising career situations) who have hitherto been excluded from jobs or relegated to undesirable jobs. This must be accomplished at the same time that promotional opportunities at the junior levels will be restricted because of the unusually large number of young people of the baby boom generation who have joined the work force in recent years and who will continue to enter the labor market through the 1980s. Management must, therefore, develop and employ improved methods for motivating employees and sustaining their morale. Moreover, management must continue to seek new methods for increasing productivity. Problems in this area have aroused substantial concern among observers of the U. S. economy in recent years. In the view of some of the contributors to this book, these problems will constitute a major challenge in the decade to come.

Improving productivity

A better life in the workplace

The concern that many of this country's leaders have felt in recent years about the productivity problem is manifested in a variety of ways. One of the most prominent was the initiative taken several years ago to establish a government-sponsored and supported research organization. This body would investigate specific issues related to productivity and make proposals for resolving these problems. As a result, the National Center for Productivity and Quality of Working Life was set up. Dr. William Batt, former chairman of the center, feels serious concern about productivity trends in this country.

"We could measure productivity by capital; we could measure productivity by technology; we could measure productivity by energy or miles per gallon; but the Bureau of Labor Statistics thinks in people terms, so we measure productivity of the workers. Our productivity today as a society is higher than that of any other country in the world and has been for a number of years. Still, what concerns us is the *rate* of productivity increase; in our society it has gone down over the past few years. Our rate of increase has been below 3 percent and our job needs have been between 7 and 10 percent. I would hope that our productivity in this country would increase as there is greater public awareness of the need for increasing it, as we become more of a trading nation and more of general markets than we have in the past."

Batt's contention that we must improve the productivity of the American economy is strongly echoed in these comments by former President Gerald R. Ford.

"Our nation today faces problems that are unprecedented in this generation. We are being whipsawed by both inflation and recession and pressured by powerful foreign economic forces. In these troubled times it is imperative that labor, management, and government find ways of working together to bolster the strength of the American economy. At the heart of our problems is the need to improve productivity.

"The United States has long been in the forefront of the effective utilization of manpower, energy, and material resources. Our high productivity has been the source of our standard of living. In recent years, however, American productivity dropped below the average of the past two decades and fell short of its great potential. We must focus now on ways to achieve higher levels of productivity so that labor's real earnings can increase again. The maintenance of our historic rate of productivity growth is a vital factor in the broader task of achieving a less inflationary and more stable economy.

"Enhancing the quality of the work environment is closely related to productivity improvement. As the material status of people improves we should give more attention to those qualitative aspects of working lives. A more satisfying work environment is a worthy goal in itself. It can also benefit all by helping to increase productivity."[5]

President Ford's comments indicate that the issue of work life quality is directly linked to productivity. A number of the other respondents also discussed the interrelated questions of employee motivation, morale, and career development. In some instances their comments, like those of President Ford, link the motivation and morale issues directly to the question of productivity. Others explored motivation and morale independently of other subjects. In either case, however, many of the respondents' observations on motivation, morale, and career development have a direct bearing on productivity.

Too many workers?

A survey of these observations may begin with a review of the comments offered by Walter Gerken, chairman of the board of Pacific Mutual. According to Gerken, one key to successful staff development is rotation, providing employees with regular opportunities to move into new job situations and new challenges. Yet these shifts cannot always come via promotions, for reasons already noted. Gerken contends that we must therefore imbue organizations with new attitudes toward job shifts, attitudes that encourage staff members to take advantage of transfer opportunities even when no promotion is involved.

"I believe that we need to take the stigma out of rank in a corporation, That is to say, if a person steps from a higher spot to a lower spot on the hierarchy, it is not necessarily a diminishing move in his or her eyes or in the eyes of co-workers. We need to make the work place fulfill both a person's creativity and changing needs in life. It is my own perception that no matter what the job is, if people are in it too long they will actually go stale. People like to be renewed and given new challenges."

A proper system of rotating employees between and among jobs in patterns different from the traditional vertical mobility model may therefore offer some promise for increasing worker productivity. Several other commentators who discussed the employee motivation issue offered provocative suggestions. These suggestions should be of interest to managers facing the motivation and productivity questions. In fact, the analysis these respondents offer represents a *double challenge*: Managers must not only prevent the lack of promotion opportunities from bringing about further productivity losses; the strategies that managers develop for dealing with limited advancement opportunities must, at the same time, support efforts to increase productivity. In this connection we turn to the challenging and provocative analysis offered by the late Blackburn Hazlehurst, former chairman of Hazlehurst & Associates, an employee benefit and actuarial consulting firm.

Like Gerken, Hazlehurst's assessment of the employment situation places considerable emphasis on what Hazlehurst labels the "vertical ascendency" model—that is, the process by which good performance is rewarded by ever-increasing responsibility, authority, and compensation. Similarly, Hazlehurst suggests that giving up the "vertical ascendency" model may not necessarily preclude improvements in productivity and worker effectiveness.

"Our society may well have developed to a point where a vertical ascendency through a corporate structure seeking more and more perquisites, greater financial resources, and more recognition may not be the best route to satisfaction, much less to effectiveness. Longer-lasting personal satisfaction might be fostered by a system that stresses the rewards of meeting a challenge suited to the individual without stressing so much the view that some people are better because they are facing a bigger challenge or a different kind of challenge."

Quite obviously, the vertical mobility model is prevalent, particularly among executives and professionals. This will make any rapid transition to the approach Hazlehurst suggests difficult under any circumstances. Nevertheless, in view of the increasing numbers available for promotion, employees may have real incentives to join with management in developing new systems of reward and motivation. In fact, Caroline Bird, author of *The Case Against College* and a number of other social commentaries, argues that a time will soon come when the number of promotable workers far outnumber the higher-level positions available.

"The supply of talent vis-à-vis promotion possibilities will be so overwhelming it will be hard to maintain the fiction that promotions are based on objectively measured merit. Equity will become so insistent a demand that managers may be urged to select among equally qualified candidates on the basis of a lottery or auction. Promotions go to the lowest bidder."

Even if advancement opportunities don't quite dwindle in relation to candidate supply in the extreme fashion that Bird foresees, it is beyond question that the trends she and others have identified are already present and will continue into the coming decade. We will be faced with the challenge of redirecting worker expectations regarding promotion and making possible greater productivity increases.

One simple and obvious first step toward developing and implementing such a strategy would be to start counseling workers on the job about the impact that demographics are continuing to have on promotion possibilities. One respondent, George Sherman, management consultant on productivity and employee efficiency systems, reported that he came away from a visit to Japan very much impressed with the system managers use in that country to stay in contact with employee problems.

"The Japanese practice a form of TLC, that puts us in a category of second raters. If you think that I mean TLC as meaning 'tender loving care,' I don't. In the Japanese approach to management, TLC stands for 'training, listening, and communicating.' Training is a way of life in the Japanese industry, and it goes on in every level in an organization, much of it on company time but also an appreciable amount on individual time. Japanese managers and executives have learned the value of listening—listening to their employees and capitalizing on the knowledge that every worker has about his or her job.

"I happen to believe that all of us involved in industry in this great country of ours are sitting on an untapped gold mine. We have a huge resource of knowledge and information out there just waiting for us to cultivate. The third element of Japanese management success is in communication. They have an elaborate communication network, and here again, they outperform us in every aspect. I think that communications is one of the greatest problems in our world today—between nations and between individuals. This is one of the most serious problems we have."

The challenge Sherman offers management today is to become much more active in training, listening, and communicating. In terms of what we learned about the likely composition of the work force in the 1980s and 1990s, the effective contacts between workers and management that Sherman envisions must include detailed orientation. Younger managerial personnel in particular must be made aware of the advancement limitations that will very likely be a salient feature of work life in the remaining portion of this century. The strengthened worker-management ties that Sherman recommends can enhance this orientation process in several ways. First, it would help management establish credibility so that its pronouncements about advancement limitations will be more readily accepted. Second, these same strengthened ties would provide a context in which managers and workers at all levels in any organization will be able to define alternative methods for achieving both professional satisfaction and heightened productivity.

The broadened worker outlook

Limited advancement is, however, only one of the problems managers will have to confront in the area of employee motivation. At a more fundamental level, there is the question of employee satisfaction, irrespective of position in the firm or prospects for advancement. J.S. Webb, vice-chairman of the board of TRW, offered some detailed comments on this question.

"First of all, workers are becoming bored with repetitive jobs. Alcoholism, emotional problems and absenteeism are soaring today. All employees resent any impersonal treatment. Perhaps during the Great Depression just having a job was enough. But that isn't true any longer. Except in the worst times within the economy, it is found to be more difficult to recruit and hold employees for low-level repetitive jobs than for higher paying positions.

"Employees have changed their priorities. Pay used to lead the list of employee surveys followed closely by working conditions and benefits. Today pay is fifth. Job satisfaction and social impact are way up. Inflation doesn't seem to alter it and, in fact, it may even heighten concerns with the nonfinancial aspects of the job. More leisure time is wanted. People will no longer work 12 hours a day, six days a week. Many won't even work overtime when they are offered three times their pay. Employees want more understanding and a voice in running the businesses in which they are employed. Today, they question orders and will no longer accept 'Do it because I say so.' Workers who are also stockholders are finding that by pooling their proxy votes they can have a bigger say in management. Employees want less rigidity in work hours and dress."

Webb therefore joins several of the other commentators cited in this section in identifying conditions that can have an impact, adversely, on both employee morale and career interests, as well as productivity. Webb does, however, identify several examples of efforts that companies have undertaken to improve employee motivation and that also helped improve worker output.

"In Europe, Volvo and Saab automobiles are no longer built on an assembly line. A group of workers form one team and they build an individual car. The trend away from the assembly line has gone so far that in France, for example, there was a commission assigned the sole task of looking into a proposal to abolish assembly lines in that country altogether. Motorola's 'Pageboy' equipment is built the same way, with a team.

"A number of other companies have done interesting things in the way of job enrichment. The Pacific Telephone and Telegraph Company used to have employees handle complaints according to the nature of the complaint. For example, one worker used to do nothing but handle billing complaints, while another handled nothing but equipment breakdown complaints. Then they began assigning each worker an area; they said, in effect, 'You are responsible for all of Santa Monica and any complaints that come in from that area come in to you.' They found that the workers took much more pride in their work. Proctor and Gamble did away with most of their floor supervisors and made the workers on the floor responsible for ordering material, incoming inspection, seeing that goals were achieved, measuring their performance against those goals, checking the quality of the finished product, etc. Their production went up almost 35 percent. I see an increasing trend towards this type of management, where worker teams are given responsibility to set goals and then to decide how they are going to achieve the goals they themselves have established."

In addition to pursuing job enrichment and seeking to change attitudes toward promotion, management can also attempt to encourage productivity gains through altered compensation schemes. Several of the participants, Webb among them, commented on the compensation issue. Webb suggests very strongly that improved performance is not likely to be gained through compensation arrangements that simply bind staff members to their organizations.

"What I call the golden handcuff era has ended. That is the period that we have gone through for the last 50 to 75 years. Companies, in effect, have handcuffed their employees to them by various types of benefit programs. The longer you stay with a firm, the more your benefits tie you down. You lose your freedom and mobility. I believe that companies are going to learn by the middle of the 1980s that they are going to have to hold employees by using job satisfaction and job enrichment, not with golden handcuffs."

On the other hand, Edward J. Feeney of Feeney Associates believes that business has not been sufficiently imaginative with its use of compensation programs to stimulate greater productivity. (Feeney Associates is a performance improvement corporation utilizing a science called behavior modification to measurably improve work performance.)

"Our wage and incentive programs are badly designed in almost every organization. This is because the laws of human behavior are not widely known. For example, salesmen who are paid a commission on a monthly basis will typically send in two or three times as many orders the last week of the month as in any other week. This follows one of the laws of human behavior that states that the frequency of our behavior increases just before the known payoff time occurs. This phenomenon in any organization can be predicted and can be amazingly accurate. What we have to do for tomorrow in our society is to make the payoff time unpredictable. I see new market packages introduced on a contingency basis to be earned when performance is improved and sustained."

Thomas Paine, whose views on discrimination against female workers have already been noted, does not believe that any large-scale new pay schemes that link output to compensation will materialize in the near future.

"The pay system in our country for hourly, salaried, and executive individuals does not do a good job in relating compensation to productivity. Most do not differentiate significantly between marginal and very good performance. This is partly because unions have bargained for pay by the hour rather than by unit of output, but I also see the same pattern where there are no unions. Maybe companies are more comfortable not differentiating. Many line managers feel partially responsible if one of their work team is not doing well. They support the inefficient and squash the brilliant and tend to pay people more in a broad middle path. Pay can be a very significant incentive device, but we don't seem to be administering it to accomplish that objective."

Nevertheless, Paine does not rule out the possibility of change entirely.

"I do see certain things starting to happen. Experiments with methods of doing production work are underway and will grow more prevalent. We will also experiment with new ways of paying people instead of following the old ways. As we learn to organize work differently, rearrange work time, and encourage participation in decision making, pay systems will also change to be better oriented towards productivity."

Perhaps the experiments can also provide further insight into the feasibility of the innovative pay arrangements that observers such as Feeney have proposed for consideration.

Programs to raise productivity

The respondents' comments thus suggest possible ways in which efforts to enhance motivation and assist in career development may aid in improving productivity. To a lesser extent, altering pay schemes may also be relevant to productivity improvement, although the comments on this score seem less conclusive. In completing this chapter, we will look at several additional suggestions on productivity issues, which may offer insight about how productivity increases can be accelerated. These comments focus on the possibility of establishing formal programs that are specifically designed to increase the productivity of individual businesses. The first of the commentators whose remarks will be reviewed in this connection is Dr. C. Jackson Grayson, founder of the American Productivity Center in Houston, Texas.

Dr. Grayson argues that management should attempt to enlist workers in cooperative efforts explicitly tailored to increasing productivity at the work site.

"Regarding productivity, one of the best ways to begin is to form a group, a nucleus of employees and managers working together. Some people call these labor-management productivity teams. The name isn't important. What is important is the idea that productivity starts right here with us. We have to think of ways to improve what we do. People have to be brought together.

"Great nations can make a choice between progress or decay. An economist once made the point that when a ship is sinking you don't have to stand there, you can do something. Even if I say that the productivity rate of the United States is declining and that our economic ship of state is in trouble, we still have options. One thing we can do is to stand there and moan our fate, and drink as the ship settles beneath the waves. The other thing we can do is man the pumps, repair the leaks, find out what the problems are and sail on. So we do have a choice."

How likely is it that the sorts of worker-management cooperation Dr. Grayson advocates can actually come about? Thomas Paine, we will recall, cited a number of instances in which the allocation of increased responsibility to workers resulted in greater output. Equally relevant to this issue are the comments of I.W. Abel, former president of the United States Steel Workers.

"Take a look at the area and problem of productivity. The steel workers union has been concerned with the industry situation regarding both imports and productivity. . . . We incorporated a provision in our 1971 collective bargaining settlement that established the joint union-management advisory committee to devise means of improving productivity and promoting the use of domestic steel. Productivity for many years has improved and has been improved in the proper manner and for mutual benefits. Unions have helped to stabilize a vital basic industry and in helping to improve productivity we believe that our union has added another dimension to its continuing constructive role in a free society."[6]

The role of organized labor

Is the sort of cooperation Abel cited possible in other labor-management situations? A glance at some of the comments other respondents offered about the future posture of the trade union movement does not seem immediately encouraging. Dr. Henry Duncombe, former economist with General Motors, is among the skeptics.

"Labor in the United States has historically adhered to—and I believe still largely does—to the old Samuel Gompers conception of labor as being concerned with wages and working conditions. Generally speaking, the organized labor view has been one of an advocate. I think that this is still the overwhelming view of most U.S. labor leaders. They view themselves as advocates. In the early trucking negotiations it is an advocacy type of bargaining that goes on. You can contrast this with other views within the labor movement, particularly the development of the movements in Europe today, where there are the labor unions pushing for participation in corporate policy-making groups. This is a change. The concept of advocacy has given way to the concept of shared control. The notion of codetermination is very much on the front burner in Germany. But it is also an integral part of a corporate law applicable to the Common Market as a whole. And the notion of shared control is really quite different from the one the American labor movement has grown up with. The primary focus of American labor over the next five to ten years still is going to be advocacy, and it is still going to be the bread-and-butter issues of hours, wages, and working conditions. There will be really very little ideological content to it."

Similarly, William Winpisinger, president of the International Association of Machinists, argues that the advocacy or adversarial relationship between labor and management is proper and should be encouraged.

"Being militant in the proper direction is what this country needs a hell of a lot more of. People are going through all sorts of things today, trying to generate new ideas about conflict resolution, worker participation in management, the suppressing of worker participation. I view all of that with a very broad distaste. It works fine in some societies. But here in this society it doesn't work because we lack that kind of social structure at the moment. The only way to carve it out and get it there is to be more militant and constructive at the same time. I have always said that if the adversary system is good enough to form the underpinning for our Anglo-Saxon system of jurisprudence, then it ought to be good enough to achieve justice on the job. I don't think that you do the best job for your constituency unless you work in an adversary relationship. Certainly there is nothing wrong with doing your best, it seems to me, whichever side of the table you happen to be sitting on! I don't see any of the businessmen trying to reduce adversary relationships in business; just to the unions."

Do the prediction and prescriptions of continued (or increased) adversarial dealings between organized labor and management necessarily preclude greater union-management collaboration on productivity? Not necessarily. It is true, of course, that the sort of increased militancy that Winpisinger advocates can limit the union's energies strictly to seeking greater benefits and compensation for workers. "Militancy" can have other broader meanings, however. For example, it is certainly possible to link pay and benefit increases to increased productivity. Enlightened labor leaders like Winpisinger are concerned with both maintaining the strength of unions and improving this country's capacity to compete with our trading partners. The challenge to them to work with management to increase productivity may be a welcome invitation. Joining in such an effort will help them achieve their own organization goals more readily.

The role of business

Winpisinger and his colleagues in union leadership are certainly not the only persons to whom a "challenge" about productivity improvements must be issued. There is also a need for attitude changes in the business community. Without these changes very little progress can be expected on the productivity front.

Dr. Milton L. Rock of Hay Associates, an international consultant company in the management of human resources, focused on the need for greater encouragement and tolerance of risk in the development of new products and services. Product development efforts are obviously relevant to the productivity question.

"The problems associated with limited productivity increases cannot be solved without experimental and innovative efforts. But such efforts are unlikely to emerge when management is dominated by a basic attitude of timidity in product and service development. A dramatic change has occurred in large American businesses that can get a quick, almost guaranteed return on the things they know they can do well: they are less willing to invest in innovative and risky kinds of products. Even compensation programs in such companies reinforce this mentality: people get rewarded for short-term returns from safe investments. Even the boards of directors reinforce this trend. The public, too, is unwittingly supporting it by saying, 'Why do you have such large debts?' Finally, the banks are unwilling to invest in people who are poor risks even though these are the people who could come up with new products.

"I think there are serious implications for the remainder of this century if this pattern continues. It is the antithesis of what we really want. We want the large debt, we want the write-off. If we expect to grow, it is only in taking these risks that we can get into new arenas. As a society, we ought to have the risk element. But if we have no write-offs and if the public cries out for conservatism, then the risks will come to an end. An overly conservative approach to business planning and management will have a negative result."

As Rock indicated, an overly conservative approach to business planning and management can have a negative effect on an organization's capacity to develop new products and services. In addition, it can definitely limit management's capacity to deal in an innovative manner with problems such as those that inhibit productivity.

The comments offered by Keizo Saji, chairman and president of Suntory Limited, are instructive on this point.

"Looking into the 1980s, I believe that the most crucial problem confronting business is how we may be able to identify and develop the vitality of business. Vitality in a business originates from taking responsible risks. Dependency and over-reliance upon government should be replaced by untiring attempts toward innovation and development on every front if a business is to survive through the 1980s as an ongoing concern."

Lack of resourcefulness and innovative spirit can have an adverse impact on productivity and this country's competitive posture. This is clearly, if rather mournfully, illustrated by episodes a few years ago involving New England commercial fishermen who were being run out of business by Russian fisherman. Large Russian vessels were equipped to process and pack quickly the yield delivered to them around the clock by shifts of fishermen. A superior product was finished and ready for delivery when the vessel returned to port. Our American stalwarts of the free enterprise system were pleading for the extension of U.S. territorial waters so their fishing could be protected. Nobody suggested that our fishermen streamline their own operation, devise more efficient technology, and attempt to offer the market a superior product at a competitive price. Capitalism? Our Russian neighbors were beating them at their own game!

I do not, of course, mean to single out the New England fishing industry for special criticism. The

Russian trawlers that proved to be such formidable opponents are heavily subsidized by the Russian government. Moreover, other countries have extended their territorial limits as far as the New England fishermen sought to have the U.S. territorial waters expanded. And certainly there are other industries in this country that have sought government assistance rather than come up with a market-dependent, competitive product or service based on profit objectives.

The fishing episode is cited simply because it illustrates the antithesis of the attitude that will be needed to solve the major problems associated with producing productivity increases. Certainly, these problems will not be easily overcome. Nevertheless, their difficulty is exceeded only by their importance. These critically significant issues cannot be successfully addressed if the spirit of business is one of diffidence and timidity.

The prospects for change

The conclusions in earlier sections were referred to as my own. Actually, these findings seem to be, for the most part, the inescapable results of the assessments offered by the respondents rather than any creation for which I can take any special credit.

First, and most obviously, the executive level of the work force in the 1980s is going to be populated by far more women and minorities than ever imagined in the past. Second, at all levels, work-force participants are likely to demand their rights more, tolerate authoritarian supervision less, and be more committed to values and goals that extend beyond those associated with the work experience.[6] The country is facing a tremendous problem in figuring out how to increase the productivity of its work force and upgrading the facilities they depend upon to generate our nation's goods and services. In dealing with these issues, managers, it seems to me as well as many of the respondents, must first acknowledge their interrelatedness.

Second, managers must decide whether they are going to use the numerous links between productivity and personnel issues to their advantage or whether these relationships will be allowed to create additional problems for those who must manage and direct the nation's business organizations.

To state the problem in this way, of course, gives away my bias. I firmly believe that the productivity and work-force questions must be addressed jointly. It is an unprecedented opportunity, which dangles well within the grasp of the U.S. business community. What is the essence of this opportunity? Basically, it is the chance to use the talent, the motivation, and the special expertise of the "new arrivals" in the work force—women and minority group members. They are just beginning to enter the management ranks and they will occupy more and more positions in the management community during the 1980s, providing a wonderful opportunity to increase the productivity of American business. By denying advancement opportunities to women and minorities in the past, business denied itself access to all that those people could contribute toward making our businesses more productive and profitable. The 1980s will offer increasing opportunities to take advantage of all that the new arrivals can contribute.

There is no guarantee, of course, that business will take this opportunity. The business community may, through shortsightedness and lack of understanding, allow the business community to view the expanded career aspirations of women and minority group members as obstacles. Rather than looking creatively for ways in which to incorporate the special skills and experiences of the new arrivals into the search for increased productivity, business may choose certain strategies that ignore all that women and minorities have to offer in helping define and develop new products and services, new methods of production and service delivery, new markets, and new marketing techniques. The results that my recommendations will yield cannot, of course, be declared with certainty. But I am very confident that the new arrivals can advance the effort greatly to secure productivity gains. However, it is with certainty that such gains will either not be achieved at all or, if achieved, in shrunken fashion if not pursued in full partnership with those who have been for so long excluded from real participation in business leadership. I hope that all of my colleagues and associates in business will seize upon this unique opportunity to improve business community performance and, at the same time, enable many thousands of skilled women and minorities to fulfill long-denied career goals and aspirations.

5

Energy

What is an energy problem?

A theme that runs consistently through the assessment of the various topics addressed in this book is the need for a better definition of important problems and concepts—what is a multinational corporation? What is free enterprise? What is corporate social responsibility? The reader should not be surprised that a discussion of the "energy problem" begins by noting that a working definition of the "problem" is required before any sort of solution can be devised. The obstacles to the development of such a definition are, however, difficult to exaggerate. Although a few suggestions about the elements that will form such a working definition will be offered, a great deal of additional effort must be expended before a usable definition of the "energy problem" is fully established. Therefore the first section introduces but does not solve the question of definition.

In large measure, the energy problem has arisen because of the changing ground rules under which the United States has obtained and used energy resources.[1] Indigenous supplies of relatively cheap energy resources used to satisfy the nation's needs on which the United States has come to depend are getting scarcer. At the same time, energy consumption is increasing. These developments were emphasized by former Representative Thomas Ashley (D-Ohio), chairman of the House Ad Hoc Committee on Energy, as he opened the debate in August 1977 on legislative proposals developed in response to President Carter's energy program.

"Today the energy future of our nation is very uncertain and very insecure. It is uncertain because of the widening gap between energy supply and demand in the United States and it is dangerously insecure because of increasing reliance on foreign oil to bridge this gap. Americans—the Congress included—have been slow to realize that our domestic production of oil and natural gas peaked in the early 1970s and has been on the decline since that time. Only about one out of every two Americans realizes that we import oil and only one out of ten understands that these imports now constitute nearly 50 percent of the oil we consume.

"But the facts are there and they present dangers which are undeniable. This heavy and increasing reliance on insecure foreign sources of oil poses a constant and growing threat to our domestic economy and to the security of our country. The threat comes not alone from the possibility of higher OPEC prices, another embargo, or the ability of an enemy to interdict foreign oil supplies destined for the United States. It comes as well from the certain knowledge that world production of oil will peak sometime within the 1980s and that, thereafter, world supplies will increasingly fall short of world demand. For the United States this means that even without higher OPEC prices, an embargo, or interdiction, there simply would not be, as there is now, the availability of foreign oil to bridge that widening gap between our own production and consumption of oil and natural gas.

"This is what the energy crisis is all about. Today, our factories are producing, crops are being harvested, homes are air-conditioned, and there is ample gasoline for summer vacation trips. Yet, our energy supplies are dangerously insecure and in the absence of prompt and decisive action will become more so with each month and year that passes.

"The choice we face is clear. We can rob the nation of options now available by deluding ourselves that the energy problem is of no urgency, and by so doing invite the economic disruption and peril to our security that could thrust upon us from external sources. Or we can adopt policies now which allow time for our economy to make an orderly transition from an era of cheap energy resources to one which inevitably will be more costly."[2]

Many of former Representative Ashley's observations were echoed by former representative John Anderson (R-Ill.).

"Our country has been blessed with ample supplies of easily obtained oil and natural gas. When those first discoveries were made a century ago and as the clear advantages of oil and natural gas over other fossil fuels such as coal became clear, as oil and gas rapidly began to displace fuels that we found were not as convenient, not as clean, and not as easily transportable, in addition we discovered a wide range of other uses for these new sources of energy.

"By far, the largest uses of the two fuels that I have mentioned, oil and gas, were in the field of transportation. Oil and gas also found extensive uses in the industrial field. And finally, they became virtually indispensable for the heating and the cooling of millions of American homes, offices, and commercial establishments.

"The industry that produced oil and gas was able to find ample supplies of this form of energy and to get it to market cheaply. Only in 1965 did our excess capacity for producing oil fall below our imports.

"However, since that time we have seen a very, very rapid disintegration in the situation to the point where we have come all the way to a place where virtually 50 percent of our consumption of oil is coming from imported oil.

"What has also happened during the years past, which I have all too briefly described, is that the American people and American industry have been accustomed to low prices. . . . Over the years we have, as a result, drawn down our reserves of oil and gas very rapidly. We were able to find enough each year to provide the kind of supply-and-demand balance that kept prices either stable or even trending downward.

"It is clear, however . . . that this era of cheap and abundant energy has ended. We cannot expect to find within the borders of this great nation of ours the kind of supplies at the cost at which we have been able in the past. New supplies will be available. I believe that new supplies must be developed, but it is going to be at a higher cost; and this is the crux of our energy policy problem. The problem is basically one of balancing expectations with reality. While we might expect to be able to continue our wasteful and, yes, even our prodigal ways, the reality of our energy supply profile today is that we cannot rest content in the same old way; and the longer we procrastinate in making necessary decisions to change our ways, the more danger there is that we will move our country into a position where we will face truly monumental problems in national security as well as economic problems of untold magnitude."[3]

In the view, therefore, of former Representatives Ashley and Anderson, and of many other commentators, this country must either continue to become increasingly dependent on foreign energy suppliers or initiate a program that somehow combines the conservation of energy with the development of alternate energy resources, most of which are currently not considered economically feasible. For example, a lowgrade form of petroleum, called "heavy oil" or "gunk," is available in huge quantities in the United States. However, it is seldom used because it cannot be extracted, refined, and marketed at competitive prices. (This is not to suggest, of course, that foreign oil is particularly cheap or that it will get any cheaper in the years to come.)

Another often recommended strategy is to increase the use of certain energy resources that raise special environmental concerns—for example, nuclear energy or coal from strip mines. Once again, however, cost factors must be considered. Such costs are either inflicted on the public at large through damage to the environment (if the resources are used with minimum safeguards) or on the consumer (if more costly safeguards—e.g., "scrubbers," which "clean up" the smoke generated by burning coal—are employed).

The extent and exact nature of the "energy problem" can be abstractly defined if we address the following questions. How can we insure that the United States maintains access to enough usable energy resources to support (and expand?) its economic production and distribution capacities? And how can this be achieved without making the nation unduly vulnerable to hostile actions on the part of foreign suppliers and without ruining the nation's water, air, and other natural resources.[4] In these questions, the notion of reasonable cost is subsumed under the rubric of supporting and/or expanding the country's economic base. The economic base is not "supported" nor can it be "expanded" if the price paid for energy resources consumes such a share of the nation's income that no investment capital is available for other uses, that the standard of living plummets, etc.

Above, it was noted that the energy problem could be "abstractly" defined using certain terms and concepts. Naturally, however, the problem cannot be concretely defined until and unless there is some operational definition given to each of the individual terms. For example, there must be some determination of the desired levels of economic activity, the energy needed to sustain (expand?) those activities, the degree of vulnerability of foreign suppliers the United States is willing to tolerate, and so forth. Making these determinations will not be easy, but decisions on these issues are needed before any solutions to the energy problem can be developed and implemented.[5]

An overview of the problem

All of the topics analyzed in this book are pressing issues. However, the energy problem was probably the focus of more immediate concern than any other subject the respondents addressed. A number of factors accounted for this concern. First, the petroleum shortages that occurred during and after the 1973 Middle East crisis had a lasting impact on many Americans, including leaders of Congress and key members of the executive branch. Subsequently, Congress and the President enacted a series of laws designed to resolve the problems that had been identified in the course of the Arab oil embargo and its aftermath.[6] Despite the impressive scope of these enactments, leading policymakers (including those responsible for energy policy in the Carter Administration) believed the new laws failed to come to grips adequately with the entire range of issues and questions associated with the energy problem. Hence, during the initial interviewing period for this book, there was continued discussion related to the energy problem, a discussion that involved both the nation's political leaders and many articulate activists. This discussion not only reflected the ongoing concerns many Americans felt for the energy problem. It also helped reinforce that concern. For example, a severe winter in 1978, which resulted in heating fuel shortages, inflated utility bills, and physical hardships for many of the nation's citizens, underscored the need many Americans felt for a more effective national energy policy.

It was against the background of the widespread concern over these diverse developments that President Carter proposed what he styled a comprehensive energy program. It was designed to deal with such issues as wasteful consumption, overdependence on foreign suppliers, and increasing fuel costs.[7] The President's program attracted widespread attention, if not overwhelming approval, in Congress, the media, and the business and labor communities. The unveiling of President Carter's program had the effect of intensifying the debate over the energy problem, a debate that had continued since the Arab boycott.

America's greatest problem?

None of the respondents who dealt with energy-related issues downplayed their significance. Two in particular, an elected official and a trade union leader, signaled out the energy problem as the most pressing difficulty this country faces in the coming decade.

The views of William Winpisinger, president of the International Association of Machinists, have been cited on several occasions, touching on such subjects as effective policies toward multinational corporations and the role of adversary bargaining in labor-management relations. In Winpisinger's opinion, the energy problem will be the chief factor determining the course taken by the American economy in the coming decade.

"Without question the number one influence on the economy in the 1980s and 90s is the energy situation and the kinds of decisions that are made. The nation is probably at the critical decision-making stage now. We probably should have made some of these decisions already, if not all of them. In a way, I am glad that we didn't make all of them. There are some things in the picture that are being totally ignored out of what may be

legislative ignorance or out of the fact that no one
has been able to encapsulate what needs to be considered. No one has devised the kind of package
that I think it merits.

In a later section of this chapter we will have
occasion to examine some of the specific proposals
Winpisinger recommends for dealing with energy-related issues. For the moment, however, we
will consider the views of Representative Wyche
Fowler, Jr. (D-Ga.). Fowler's view on the importance of the energy problem closely parallel Winpisinger's.

"I do think that the chief question in the world
today is one of resources. We are simply, as a nation, not going to be able to maintain the levels of
consumption that we have experienced in the last
30 or 40 years. Most people don't like to talk about
it because they always end up sounding like
doomsdayers if they talk about the limits on Fossil
fuels and the limits on nonrenewable resources in
the world."

To argue that energy-related problems constitute *the* single most critical economic issue facing
the United States is to offer a powerful and sweeping declaration. There are, after all, many other
pressing problems with which U.S. leaders in both
the public and private sectors must continue to
grapple. Questions such as how to improve the
government's regulatory program, the best methods for increasing productivity, and a proper understanding of the social responsibility that private business must discharge pose significant
challenges. Yet any substantial disruption of the
nation's effort to obtain adequate supplies of energy resources at manageable prices will surely in-
flict untold damage on the production and distribution of goods and services. In addition, there
are profound foreign policy consequences to consider. A disruption of energy supplies might,
through confrontation with Arab oil producers,
cause a general deterioration of the Middle East

situation. It could even cause direct conflict between the United States and the Soviet Union.

In some circles, the energy question does not have top billing and there are those who specifically take issue with the designation of the energy problem as the nation's most critical economic challenge. In addition, the basic problem to them seems not to be an exhaustion of energy resources on Spaceship Earth; that is not the problem. Yet it is the problem on which many people focus. But, some say, Spaceship Earth will never run out of energy. At this late date in history, we have explored a relatively small percentage of the earth's surface looking for oil. Three fourths of the globe is under water, and we have only begun testing the outer continental shelf in some parts of the world and not tested at all in many parts of the world. Here in this country, we have explored underwater reserves in the Gulf of Mexico and have hardly scratched the Eastern Seaboard. So it seems that the odds would be in favor of someday finding oil fields deep underwater.

Most people today, however, assign the energy question to a place among the top five economic problems facing the country. In addition, there is a strong voice in the nation saying that the energy question is directly related to the problem of capital formation, which may be the most important economic question the United States confronts. Thus, while not everyone will agree that the energy problem constitutes the most pressing economic issue for the coming decade, we would have a difficult time challenging the significance Winpisinger and Fowler attach to that problem. Their conclusions become all the more compelling in light of the difficulties associated with addressing and solving specific energy-related issues. Those difficulties will become more evident as they are discussed in the remainder of this chapter.

The impact of the energy problem: foreign and domestic

Even to the most indifferent observer, the rather substantial increases in retail gasoline and natural gas prices since 1973 should be painfully evident. (Exact figures can be obtained from the Department of Energy's Annual Report to Congress.) Indeed, these increases may be the most constant reminders most of us experience of the enduring energy problem we face. Rawleigh Warner, Jr., Chairman of the board of the Mobil Oil Corporation, attributes the increases in petroleum prices to what he describes as the "politicization" of the price-setting process.

"You hardly need reminding of how low oil prices remained as long as they were determined by market forces and as long as the oil companies were able to bargain effectively with the oil-exporting countries. It was only when this commodity was politicized by the oil-exporting countries, beginning a few years ago, that its price began to be manipulated by them and market forces ignored."[8]

Beyond their adverse impact on domestic retail prices, the increases in the oil prices charged by the Organization of Petroleum Exporting Countries (OPEC) have also damaged the balance-of-payments standings of many countries, including the United States. Warner also refers to this consequence of the OPEC pricing actions.

"Over and above any long-term inflationary impact of OPEC's price increases, their suddenness and their size have exerted great adverse impact on nearly every other country's balance of payments and have placed terrible strains on the international financial and monetary systems."[9]

The balance-of-payments problem is also of concern to David N. Judelson, president of Gulf + Western Industries. He looks to the future and is understandably concerned about what he sees.

"Right now, I believe our imports are 50 percent of our needs and certainly by the middle 1980s, will grow to more than 50 percent of our needs. This will have a fantastic effect on our balance of payments. For example, it would be in the magnitude of an increase of $35 billion if you just paid $15 per barrel. With inflation as the cost, it will increase our balance-of-payment deficit by $35 billion. And if the price goes to $40 dollars a barrel, it would increase the deficit by well over $100 billion. That would be considerably more than the total imports back in 1972, which were only $67 billion or $68 billion. So you can see the magnitude of that problem."[10]

The economic problems discussed so far concern both the United States and other countries. An international focus is reflected in comments by former Secretary of State Henry A. Kissinger prepared for delivery to the United Nations General Assembly in September 1975. In the course of his remarks (which were actually delivered by U.N. Ambassador Daniel P. Moynihan), Dr. Kissinger labeled the recent increases in oil prices the "most devastating blow to economic development in this decade."[11] Later in this same presentation, Dr. Kissinger cited the impact of the price hikes on efforts to combat inflation and recession, as well as to aid the nonindustrialized countries.

"This dialogue is based on an approach of negotiation and consensus, not the exercise of brute economic power to gain unilateral advantage. The enormous, arbitary increases in the price of oil of 1973 and 1974 have already exacerbated both inflation and recession worldwide. They have shattered the economic planning and progress of many countries. Another increase would slow down, or reverse, the recovery and the development of nearly every nation represented in this Assembly. It would erode both the will and the capacity in the industrial world for assistance to developing countries. It would, in short, strike a serious blow at the hopes of hundreds of millions around the world."[12]

A question of national security

Thus far the discussion has dealt exclusively with prices and their impact on international finance, economic development, and trading relationships. These are not, however, the only elements of the energy problem that occupied the attention of the respondents. Governor Edmund G. ("Jerry") Brown, Jr., of California notes the national security aspects of the problem, aspects he feels have received insufficient notice.

"An area of our national security that we don't often hear about is our growing dependency on other countries for the oil and energy that keep this economic engine of ours going. Remember those long lines a couple of years ago at your local gas station? Well, nothing has changed since then. As a matter of fact, we're importing more oil today than we were at the time of the Arab oil embargo. So that's an area of vital weakness in this country. And that's something that we ought to pay more attention to than the arcane debates about strategic weapons and overkill."[13]

In Brown's view, the security of the United States has been seriously jeopardized by the capacity of foreign powers to "put this country into a state of depression by just turning off the oil spigot."[14]

Conserve or expand?

As any of the respondents would readily acknowledge, delineating the difficulties associated with maintaining adequate energy supplies at manageable prices is an exceedingly complex task. To their considerable credit, however, each contributor ventured some specific recommendations about how at least some aspects of the energy problem can be overcome. William Winpisinger dealt directly with the price issue, which has so dominated the comments examined in this section. His interest can be stated plainly: How can lower prices be obtained from petroleum suppliers?

Price is not, however, the only focus of the respondents' recommendations. Suggestions (perhaps exhortations is a better word) were offered by some concerning the need for conservation measures. Other respondents emphasized the need for expanding energy resources. These two positions, incidentally, parallel the basic camps that have developed concerning solutions to the energy problem. President Carter, while not indifferent to the need for increasing supplies, placed greater stress on reduced consumption, especially of gasoline. President Reagan reversed the energy priorities of Carter. While proposing increases for nuclear energy, Reagan, on March 10, 1981, called for extensive cuts in solar energy, energy conservation programs, and synthetic fuel development. With the nuclear exception, Reagan's budget attempts to get government out of the way and let American industry produce more energy. For the past four years, the Carter administration and Congress relied on federal spending to encourage energy conservation and to spur the development of alternative fuels. President Reagan will rely on the economics of the marketplace. While the respondents tended to avoid voicing partisan sentiments, it will be clear from their comments which side of recent energy debates each would support.

Where we (might) go from here

Earlier, it was noted that William Winpisinger was one of two respondents whose concern about the energy problem was such that he viewed it as the number one economic challenge facing the country in the 1980s. He offered a number of very specific suggestions about how this problem can be addressed, one of which has to do with the concept of greater "leverage" by the United States in dealing with energy suppliers. Winpisinger acknowledged that more than a little risk is involved in the use of leverage. Yet he felt that, when judiciously applied, this approach may be helpful in gaining concessions from those who control petroleum supplies.

"A country that is as much in the world's mainstream of trade as the United States is ought to have some ways to exert leverage against discriminatory pricing policies, either by engaging in the same practices themselves or, perhaps, by teaming up with other producers of short-supply commodities and exerting leverage in that respect.

"When you begin to talk about exerting leverage through commodities or products in the world's market, you are talking about the very same kind of spark that created a lot of fires over the course of history. And I wouldn't want to see us tamper with that to the point of a shooting war or even a cold war. However, we can't keep turning the other cheek. Certainly we have to find some kind of balance that does the best job of keeping the American citizen whole and insulated from arbitrary gouging by oil producers. The same applies for any other commodity that is in short supply or an object of a cartel. They all have to be treated similarly. One place in which we have some leverage is agriculture. The world may be in as much danger of food shortages as we are of energy shortages. If that is so, then we are probably in a very strong, center-stage position."[15]

Those nations affected by Arab oil squeezes should confer among themselves about the possibility of "withholding food and manufactured goods" from the oil-exporting nations. Less risk but certainly more discipline is demanded by the conservation approach. It is a strategy for coping with energy problems that accepts growing scarcity of energy supplies as a long-term (perhaps permanent) condition. Each of the conservation proponents among the respondents recommended this particular alternative from his own unique perspective.

Conserve

That California's Governor Brown is among the advocates of less energy usage should surprise no one. Brown is an adherent of the "small is beautiful" approach to life. He repudiates some of the more ostentatious trappings of his gubernatorial office. (He refuses to occupy his state's imposing new governor's mansion, which now stands vacant.) His constant reiteration of the limits we face in all aspects of our personal and community experiences make him a natural spokesperson for reduced energy consumption. In remarks that reflect both his national security concern and his personal philosophy, Brown argues for proper use of energy.

"It requires a discipline. It requires a leveling with the American people. The automobile companies are going to have to make an automobile that uses less gasoline. Our factories are going to have to end their wasteful ways. Each of us in our own lives is going to have to cut down on the excessive use of energy and oil, so that this country can truly have a sense of security that is real and not dependent on a few countries far away, which we don't control."[16]

Conservation of resources is also very much a part of the energy policy recommended by Representative Wyche Fowler. He is particularly concerned that the depletion of supplies will jeopardize, and perhaps even destroy, the foundations of the nation's economic system.

"Either we are going to have to cut back very seriously, or we are going to have very drastic disruptions in an economic system that we have become accustomed to. I happen to think that there is not enough coal and oil in the world for us to maintain our industrial patterns of comsumption. Unless we are careful we will see many industries become like dinosaurs, where they simply cannot afford the energy costs to maintain production.

"Now if that happens, our whole economic system and private capitalism as we have known it in its highly industrialized state will be in jeopardy. I wish I knew what the answer was. We have had signals from more than just the oil countries. The severe weather in recent years has shown us that, in times of crisis, either man-made or natural, our reserves and our systems are very fragile. Of course, according to some people, we have a 'technology' mentality in this country. Whether you are talking about a cure for cancer or a cure for worldwide resource shortages, most people believe that science and technology will come up with that magic pill to cure whatever crisis confronts us. To put is positively, I believe that we have reached a point in the world where everything we will be doing in the next 100 or 200 years will basically depend upon what our energy resources are going to be. Until we grapple with how we, as a country, are continuing to use about a third of the world's nonrenewable resources, it is pretty hard to talk about anything else."

For former Attorney General Ramsey Clark, the question is not so much whether effective conservation measures will be applied, but rather by whom? In Clark's view the alternatives define themselves very simply: either the business community assumes direct responsibility for energy conservation or the government will. Two distinctly pessimistic themes are sounded in Clark's comments. First, there is the lamentable but indisputable fact that industry has not established a very good record in disciplining itself. Second, the long-term interests that the entire human community has in energy conservation are in conflict with the short-term interests business has in maintaining profitability.

Industry must find ways to determine public need and to discipline itself to tailor its production to that need. Otherwise, the only alternative will be government control. Clark cites the automobile industry as an example.

"It has failed to date. It has continued to avoid the voluntary assumption of responsibility to do something about emission control. Government will have to do it. Government can drag its feet only to the peril of national health. We produced more cars than babies in each of the last 10 years. The automobile industry has to begin to see itself as serving transportation needs and to see that we're a society that has a great need for mass transit. We just can't continue to pour more cars into a city like New York. There is not enough space for them. If the industry can't have the foresight to convert, if it can't have the foresight to control its energy costs, then government must.

"Take the building industry as a second example. A contractor for a major office building can cut costs on insulation and on heating and cooling systems, both at the long-range cost of much greater energy consumption. Suppose he builds the building and sells it to a buyer at a lower cost. However, the long-range cost to the buyer, and society, is an enormous use of energy. We can't go on like that. We have to be energy-conscious in all of our activities. If it costs more to insulate now to reduce energy consumption, it has to be done. If the construction industry won't recognize that, then government must. It is going to be very difficult for industry to do it because they have to look at the bottom line. And the bottom line is that an underinsulated building costs less to construct than a properly insulated building, and I am going to be able to sell it for a lower price. The same with homes or other facilities.

"Finally we have to recognize the limits of growth. It may be the hardest thing for America to do because we have had a continuing growth or frontier. All of our frontiers haven't been physical, the mountains and the Pacific, but we have this constant psychology of growth. We have to examine, and industry must voluntarily examine, the limits of growth and act in the public interest. That is a very hard lesson. But if industry doesn't take some role, then the government, through planning and regulation, will have to."

Some characteristically blunt observations on energy conservation are also offered by William Winpisinger. He sees the conservation approach as part of a larger strategy in which scarce resources are rationed, not by the price mechanism but rather by mandatory allocations. His opposition to price rationing is based on its regressivity. "I would like to see us engage in some meaningful conservation techniques and programs, something that goes beyond simple rhetoric and yet less extreme than price rationing. Price rationing is probably the easiest conservation technique to administer, but it discriminates totally against those at the bottom of the economic ladder. I think they have shared enough in the energy misery. They are the ones who, by and large, have gone without heat; by and large, they are the ones who can't afford the energy-using equipment that abounds in this society. To rob them of the use of motor vehicles, for example, because of price conservation is unconscionable. So we have to find a better way. I think that probably the only fair way is rationing. And I think that the government does have the capacity to do it if we are really serious about it."

Explore and expand

As indicated above, one of the most pressing issues that has emerged during the debates that have swirled around the energy problem since the mid-1970s concerns the degree of emphasis placed on various programs. Does the nation emphasize conservation efforts? Or does it concentrate on developing new sources of energy and/or finding additional supplies of the types now widely in use. (The term *exploration* might be an appropriate descriptor for the alternative that emphasizes searching for additional resources.)

Regardless of the term used, however, the option of forestalling energy shortages by finding and extracting additional energy supplies is advocated by many commentators, including several of the respondents. David Judelson feels that there is a markedly inadequate amount of exploration taking place at present. He attributes the shortfall to a lack of financial incentives. In Judelson's view, this has, in turn, induced the petroleum companies, which ought to have the greatest interest in exploration efforts, to invest their development funds elsewhere.

"So what are we doing? Are we taking depletion away from the oil companies? We increase, therefore, the risk in developing new reserves, which is counterproductive to the needs of the country? What do the companies do in turn? You see Mobil acquiring an interest or control in Marcor and you see Atlantic Richfield in Anaconda. They are putting their money where they think they can get a better return on an investment. I don't think they should be allowed to do that, by the way. I think they should put cash back into exploration and further development of domestic reserves. But for them to do that we have to give them back depletion allowances so that they get the cash flow that's necessary to make the risks worthwhile. But they should not be allowed to take that depletion allowance and put it into anything else other than reinvestment. Individuals as well as corporations in the oil business have taken money out and not put it back in. So rather than take the depletion allowance away, they should have forced them to take every dollar of depletion and put it back into exploration. If they would not do that, then tax the depletion allowance away from them."

Judelson's emphasis on incentives for exploration is strongly endorsed by Henry Duncombe. He recommends expanding the energy supplies available in the United States. Higher energy costs will necessarily accompany the strategy Duncombe suggests, a development he readily acknowledges. Moreover, like Governor Brown, Duncombe sees a significant "national security" consideration, which must be addressed in the effort to resolve the energy problem.

"I have long felt that one of the aspects of the energy problem that disturbed me the most is its implications for national security. I put a fairly high priority on national security and I hate to see the Congress pass a law that exposes our energy plight to the arbitrary decisions of the Mideast oil-producing countries. With respect to that issue, I would be tempted to set up special development incentives to private industry to develop our domestic resources even at a higher cost. However, I would do this with the conscious, deliberately articulated understanding (a) that it may bring higher costs but (b) that it is a cost that we may want to assume for national security reasons. As the matter stands right now, we are extraordinarily vulnerable.

"With respect to other materials, the problem is somewhat different because most of the materials are recyclable. The aluminum made from Jamaican bauxite can be recycled. The copper that comes out of Chile or Peru can be recycled. Petroleum can't be recycled, however. Frankly, while I recognize the possibility of bauxite or copper cartels, I am not so concerned about them as I am in the petroleum area. I could certainly, on the grounds of national security, endorse a special program, despite higher costs, if that is the price of getting national security. That is a very special problem."

The energy problem in the 1980s and 90s

The House Ad Hoc Committee on Energy, in the introduction to its report on the omnibus energy legislation that it recommended to the U.S. House of Representatives in 1977, expressed the hope that the rancor and stridency that have characterized energy policy debates in the past could be avoided during consideration of the committee's proposals.[17] On the other hand, the committee was correct in its suggestion that any sudden falloff in the emotion surrounding energy-related discussions would sharply break with previous practices.

Whether Congress (and the nation as a whole) could ever adhere to the spirit of the House committee's admonition is doubtful at best. What is clear is that, rancorous or not, the debate will most assuredly continue well into this as well as the next decade.[18]

What can business leaders and other interested parties do to contribute constructively to the ongoing energy debate? First, they can accept the inescapable fact that debate will be protracted. The sheer complexity of the energy problem renders it immune to any rapid solution. Recognizing and acknowledging this fundamental fact will provide some measure of protection against the disappointments and frustrations. Setbacks are bound to result when consensus on proposed solutions eludes problem solvers and when the shortcomings of the solutions that are attempted begin to reveal themselves.

A second recommendation concerns reform of the government's regulatory apparatus. In Chapter 1 it was suggested that a vast amount of work must be done if the existing regulatory programs are to be brought together and integrated in a more acceptable way. The importance of the energy problem and the increasingly direct role government must play in addressing that problem give added emphasis to the need for regulatory reform.

The entire community, including business leadership, must contribute to reform by continuing to protest against various government regulatory efforts that duplicate and contradict each other and add needless cost to products and services. In addition, data must be supplied to government leaders interested in reform about the adverse effects of current regulatory activities. Carefully crafted solutions must be formulated and supported by the business community. The key to the whole effort is first to establish broad goals for the regulatory effort, then to assess current practices and proposed improvements in that context. At present, there are literally thousands of types of regulatory activities going on at once with little coordination and without any sort of broad economic objectives. Business can thus contribute to solving (or at least ameliorating) the energy problem by supporting constructive attempts to improve the government's overall regulatory program.

Earlier, reference was made to the debate between the "conservationists" and the "explorationists." It is unclear how or even if that debate will be resolved. (If it is resolved, it will likely be a draw, since many of the programs that each side advocates will be necessary in order to create an effective solution.) However, one result of the country's concern with the energy problem will be a noticeable alteration of life-styles. For example, those members of the business community whose endeavors depend upon or substantially involve use of internal combustion engines and gasoline should make especially intense preparations for change. They will have to produce and/or use more fuel-efficient equipment and identify substitutes for petroleum products or the devices that use such products. In the recreational field an increased interest is already evident in such non-gas-guzzling activities as hiking, biking, jogging, rafting, and backpacking. In years to come, activities of this sort will probably receive even greater attention in comparison with motorboating, water-skiing, "pleasure" aviation, and touring by "recreational vehicles." Planners in the recreation industry must obviously take into account these trends as they prepare themselves and their organizations for the business environment of this decade. Other sectors of the economy will probably be effected by similar developments and must plan accordingly.

The tone of this chapter has been rather somber, at times downright negative. This is probably unavoidable. There are not many elements of the energy problem that lend themselves to lighthearted or casual treatment. Nevertheless, there is at least one aspect of the problem that should excite positive feelings.

One of the greatest difficulties associated with the energy problem is that no widely accepted alternatives have been identified that could replace the types of energy resources and energy-dependent equipment and facilities now in use. Nuclear energy, for example, will have to be under scrutiny for a considerable time period before issues about the safety of this particular energy source are fully resolved.

Modern history, however, provides a number of illustrations of the impact that technological advances can have upon the creation of new industries and whole new ways of life and upon the drastic alteration of existing practices. The development of the automobile, the design and use of which will doubtless be altered significantly in the 1980s, is everyone's favorite example of how technological advances can dramatically change the course of a nation's economy. Ironically, automobiles now contribute to a problem that must be solved. Photocopying and transistors have also had dramatic effects creating many new business opportunities. But it is too much to hope that any one development or device will magically appear and instantly solve the energy problem.

Nevertheless, some of the recommendations for making limited improvements in the energy situation may offer inviting prospects for enterprising product developers and marketers. For example, the U.S. Corps of Engineers reported to President Carter in 1977 on the potential for increased energy production offered by the literally thousands of small dams originally built to operate grist mills, control floods, and provide irrigation.[19] But the turbines required to convert these facilities for hydroelectric power production are not available from U.S. suppliers. However, it is a piece of technology that some entrepreneur may wish to investigate.

Similarly, the possibilities for developing economic fuel from "fibrous waste" are being explored by German-born physicist Robert Gunnerman. Whether Gunnerman's experiments are successful, the spirit of his investigations are worthy of emulation by other businessmen and women.[20] In short, what we can hope for is that the material and personal rewards associated with technological breakthroughs in the energy field will induce entrepreneurs of varying backgrounds to seek and develop opportunities for effective innovation.

Conclusion

A conclusion normally signifies that explicit direction and concrete answers are to be presented. But in this instance, the conclusion will instead present some new thinking or at least some new direction.

American business is the backbone of our society. Whether it be stated as such or identified as "country" or "society," American business must go forward or all will perish. This section of the book discusses those steps forward, highlighting issues or areas that must be identified.

Business

If there is any real common theme to President Reagan's economic program, it is clearly reducing the substantial burden and intrusiveness of government in the American economy. The time is certainly right to consider fundamental changes in the relationship between American business and government today. Over the past several decades,

America has seen a considerable growth in the intervention of government into the decision making of the private sector. Certainly a portion of that intervention was justified, but the intervention has noticeably contributed to the declining performance of the American business system.

Peter E. Haas, President of Levi Strauss & Co., indicates his rationale for American business to be more self-sufficient:

"In the 1980s and into the 1990s, America, with all of its varied needs and disciplines, will have to struggle to maintain as well as improve its status. Issues, such as regulations, productivity, women and minorities, are areas in which teamwork must be the rule and not the exception. America must work even closer together if it's going to be able to address itself proficiently and intelligently to these items now on the floor. The running of a business, the working with people, communicating to groups or masses, will require professional expertise heretofore not demanding of such urgency. Success has been labeled many things. Success or failure, at least in business and undoubtedly in both the public and private sectors, is going to be and really has always been, based on knowing how to interact with people. People will be the cornerstone to success or failure in the next 20 years. People will effect the bottomline. People will determine both the degree of success as well as the degree of failure. I cannot predict whether we will fail or not, but I can predict that we will fail if we don't work harder at improving where we have already been. Insecurity will have no place on the team. The team must be made up of only those who wish to work together. Working together will allow us to move successfully through the 1980s; to move into the 1990s will require a passport that includes sensitivity and responsiveness as its criteria."

The question in front of every businessman and woman today is whether we as managers wish to be honest and have our freedom or whether we wish to continue to be dishonest and policed.

Throughout the late 1970s and into this decade, the leadership from the business community has become more active in helping to solve local problems. The business community today is beginning to assist the management of cities and towns providing various degrees of leadership, helping to reduce the growth and financial burden of government in every conceivable local area. Certainly this relieves the stress on individual taxpayers and directly at least helps contribute to the free enterprise system by establishing more jobs.

The above can be translated into a well-worn identification label called *social responsibility.* Social responsibility has directly or indirectly brought about affirmative action, health and safety, educational responses to community needs, energy conservation, and so on. The business community is now beginning to understand the problems of social responsibility. And it is beginning to recognize that social responsibility is a system within many larger systems and that various complex forces are at work. At times, if not properly understood and properly designed, social responsibility can inhibit a corporation's operation. Whether it be because of the pressures of the Julian Bond's or the outspokenness of the Bradshaw's, the straw is now bent, and the responsibility of the business community can now only go forward. Minorities and women everywhere can now begin to find their seat in the front rows. Heretofore security, politics, and rhetoric were the only forces that would allow the disadvantaged to find their rightful place. Today, business leaders can help to elevate those disadvantaged employees to the rostrums of acceptance and balconies of opportunity for this decade.

This decade will encourage employees to make their voices heard and to be responsive corporate citizens. As never before, men and women from various corporate families will ban together and unite around causes that affect entire employee populations. Chief executive officers and the like will survive only by providing true leadership—by being at the helm and steering their ships as true captains. Activism will be the name of the game. Leadership that is visible and dynamic within the business community is going to be the difference between success or disaster. From this day forth the old politics and policies will be thrown aside, and big government will no longer have its close proximity to the business population. Of course the question remains, who are those leaders of today and tomorrow? Certainly those leaders of today and yesterday are quoted throughout this writing. Perhaps the leaders of tomorrow are some of those noted here. Perhaps they are still unprepared and waiting in the wings. For the first time, the business community is recognizing the need to properly train and cultivate those new crops. The business community, because of its economic philosophy and its unshakable faith in the integrity and potential of each individual, and because of its experience and its political activism, is today uniquely positioned and qualified to provide an era of economic, political, and social leadership.

The business community is being attacked on a daily basis by a powerful and insidious enemy that is cracking the very foundations of the corporation. We are in some way at war with and against ethics. People everywhere are losing faith in their government, in schools and churches, and certainly in business. There are many individuals in this book who speak loudly and often about how much they love free enterprise, our private enterprise economy; but perhaps they don't fully understand that implicit in the whole concept of capitalism is a high degree of honesty and mutual trust. Yes, of course, they do know this, but how many spoke out on this particular issue? Our success, our moving forward, will only happen and come about if we, as individuals, as a country, as a business community, have the courage and the independence to stand up, to speak out, to act, to demand honesty and responsibility from our peers, to be that role model so that ethics can be a guiding star and not be a burden.

The American business community must provide the necessary leadership to lead the United States out of its economic quagmire. Unfortunately, business leaders, perhaps nostalgic for the past, continue to think that if we only could rely exclusively on the profit and loss signals of the marketplace, everything would be fine. It is obvious, though, that we cannot survive in the current business environment unless we are sensitive to a broad range of signals: from politics, both domestic and international; from our host communities and our employees; from our churches and schools and other institutions; and of course, from our own conscience.

Throughout the history of this country various happenings have affected the insecurity as well as the security of all Americans. For example, Watergate in itself with all of its tragedy and trauma was simply a manifestation of the mores of our society. It was the opening of the Watergate door that allowed us to see the magnification of the flaws in the ethical framework that holds together our democratic system. But Watergate also showed the strength of the foundation built for us by those who founded this country. We did not lose faith in our democratic society, in the structure of our private enterprise system. But many citizens lost faith in the ways in which our system is implemented. Throughout America there is now a ferment of discontent about the lack of ethics, the lowering of moral standards, and the widespread vulgarization of our national culture. Fermentation is sometimes hard to contain when shook up. Industry in particularly, must be alert to this possibility. Our foundation is cracked, but our dedication and faith will allow our business structure to remain intact and to heal itself.

The business community must show the way out of our old adversarial relationships toward a new spirit of cooperation and compromise, which all parties exercise as appropriate self-denial. Government can stimulate efforts or it can discourage them, but experience shows that private individuals and groups are the ones who can get the job done. Many of us in business have been arguing for years that we can help make this economy produce more effectively if Washington would just get off our backs. Now our bluff has been called. We've got to deliver in terms of both our economic performance as well as our social responsibilities. If it was right to hold Jimmy Carter's regulators accountable for their actions, it is just as correct to hold Mr. Reagan's regulators accountable. The urgent need now is to make some sense out of the regulatory system, not merely to exploit the spoils of what might be a temporary political situation. The tables are turned. Now it is the critics of business who are often seen as a special interest. The American people have spoken against them at the polls—as they surely will against any business leaders that they perceive as acting out of narrow self-interests instead of broadly based concern for the national welfare. Businessmen and women now have an opportunity to take the lead in forging new cooperative relationships with government. It is time the business community stopped complaining and helped develop workable solutions to the problems of our society.

Today the business community is said to have a black eye, and in many respects it does (some people say it has *two* black eyes). But the leaders quoted here are represented because they have the opportunity and ability to erase that stigma. American business does not have to have a black eye, but it will continue to have that albatross around its neck until it begins to truly lead, until it becomes more dynamic and innovative, until it is both results-oriented and interwoven with social responsibility. The lack of enthusiasm by the business leadership to promote its successes and strengths and the continuing decay of team effort and good sound communication in all directions will continue to spoil the potential of American business. If the business community does not struggle to please and begin to move forward in a dynamic posture, then the competition of Japan, Third World industries, and young mavericks will dominate, isolate, and destroy the success of yesterday and dreams for tomorrow.

Productivity

This nation, its cities and towns, and its people are in the midst of a profound transition: from cheap to expensive energy, from an era of single- to double-digit inflation and interest rates, from one technological revolution to another, from regulation to deregulation. In addition, we are increasingly affected by events at the international level, including trade practices of other nations that militate against our goods and services abroad and even at home. It continues to go without saying that people are this nation's most underutilized resource today. If we continue to accept barriers which prevent talented individuals from achieving the most responsible levels of corporate power, we are wasting our greatest resource; the intelligence, creativity, and judgment of the individual. Can this country, this society really afford to pay such a price for discrimination? Is American business really willing to provide the receptacle for such waste? American business leaders have become too short-sighted, too bottomline-oriented, too short-term versus long-term. They are responsible for a lot of this society's problems. The Japanese are teaching us lessons in management which we knew 35 years ago and have forgotten. Progress still comes only from people. They are the real assets of all business, professional and direct-labor people alike.

If you examine the period of time between 1880 and the early 1950s, this country's annual growth and productivity was approximately .7 percent higher than in any other leading country today. And that relatively small but decisive difference contributed to making this country the economic and, subsequently, the political leader of the world. But since the early 1950s, particularly since the mid-1960s, those numbers have been reversed. In 1979 and 1980, this country actually had a net decline in productivity, and the differential of 1980 was substantially in favor of West Germany and Japan. What will this mean in terms of this country's standing in the world in 1990 or the year 2000? How will other nations perceive us? This country cannot let antiquated concepts of another age interfere with our need to rebuild America. Only by adapting our thinking to the needs of a new age are we going to meet the challenge of one of this nation's most pressing concerns—productivity.

Over the last number of years, this nation's productivity has dropped steadily and has even been negative in recent quarters. Other countries have also dropped, but not as greatly as we have. The reasons are many. There is a declining international competitiveness in some segments of U.S. industry as reflected in our lagging growth rate in productivity. Also there is increasing penetration of domestic markets by foreign producers, and production technology lags behind other countries especially in such areas as steel and coal. There is also a change in the direction of industrial innovation resulting from the mandated diversion of corporate effort from developing new products and processes to meeting other social goals, such as environmental preservation.

There are great opportunities to turn our productivity rate upward. But first we have to know how to measure productivity; what we cannot measure we cannot control. And yet the fact is that when productivity figures are published, they only represent the output of the manufacturing sector and occasionally agriculture. Service-sector productivity is normally excluded and so is the large service component of manufacturing. We are working with incomplete data. Is it any wonder that our conclusions are puzzling and contradictory?

The business community will be making a mistake if it thinks that the problem of productivity will be solved by the election of probusiness people to the Congress and the Senate and a president committed to balancing the budget and freeing business from government. Of course, it is essential to improve the investment climate in a variety of macroeconomic ways. But the battle against declining productivity must be fought bilaterally, both at the macro level of government policy and at the micro level of organizational reform. There is no greater single thief of productivity than sluggish economic growth and recession. As total output falls, then substantial economic capacity becomes idle, and plant and equipment are no longer running at their most efficient rate. Fixed overhead costs must be spread over fewer units of output. In contrast, the best productivity growth is attained when unemployment is falling and the demand is strong. As businesses expand rapidly in a healthy economy, the latest technology and equipment must be brought into use. A good example of Japan's commitment to increase productivity is their project called MUM, which is an acronym for Methodology for Unmanned Manufacturer. The objective is to design and build a totally automated batch manufacturing plant with the following specifications:

Size: 250,000 square feet.

Output: 2,000 different automative parts automatically assembled into 50 different products.

Processes: all automative including forging, casting, welding, heat treating, painting.

Funding: the government has supplied the first $117 million; six industries will supply the rest.

Personnel: total required to run the factory— 10.

Completion date: 1990.

To underscore Japan's commitment to this

overall grand objective, they already have in use many thousands of robots which are intelligent workstations; most of them have sensors, manipulators, and microcomputers. And the Japanese intend to export automatic factories. Does anybody want to bet against them? We could ask ourselves why Japanese auto workers have only six job classifications at a plant, while some of our major producers, for example, have more than 200. Or we could explore why Japanese and German industries impose less than one half the number of management layers than we normally do between the chief executive officer and the workers at the machine.

I would venture to predict that early in the 21st century, half of the people of this country will be working very hard to support the other half. I'm not clear whether that statement properly classifies as a prediction, a prophecy, or a threat; but one thing is a certainty beyond debate. The first step down the road to national economic happiness is to become once again the strong, productive, self-confident society that we were in the 1960s. This matter of productivity is so important, so very basic to our goal of an economically content society that productivity is the focal point of economic progress in the new decade. What this suggests is better use of our time, use of modern machines, and innovatively improved techniques and processes. Perhaps the answer to our competitive disadvantage is not to copy the Japanese but to adapt the best from their style and stamp it "Made in America."

The economy

Whatever happened to that American dream of owning your own home? Only 10 years ago, a family's house payment averaged a little more than a quarter or 27 cents out of each dollar earned. Today it takes considerably more than 40 cents out of every dollar of income. Today fewer than one out of 11 families can afford to buy their first home. The stakes in the fight against inflation are more than material wealth or even material comfort but whether or not Americans as a nation and as a people will retain control of their own destiny. In crises abroad we have always shown our ability to respond with steadfastness and with courage. The question is now whether we can use that same determination, that same national unity, that same national commitment, and that same partnership to the challenge of inflation.

We must chart a different course. We must increase productivity. We must make it possible for industry to modernize and to use the technology which we ourselves invented. It means putting Americans back to work. And that means, above all, bringing government spending back within government revenues. The inflation we face today is deep rooted. Its many causes have been built up over more than a decade—soaring energy prices throughout the world, declining productivity growth in our nation, and our failure in government and as individuals to live within our means. As individuals and as a nation we must begin to spend money according to what we can afford in the long run and not according to what we can borrow in the short run.

Since 1960 our government has spent $5.1 trillion; our debt has grown over $648 billion. Prices have exploded by 178 percent. How much better off are we for it all? When we measure how harshly these years of inflation, lower productivity, and uncontrolled government growth have affected our lives, we know we must act and act now. We must restore the freedom of all men and women to excel and to create, we must unleash the energy and genius of the American people whose traits have not failed us before. Many Americans today appear to be convinced that the economic problems of the nation are manufactured in Washington by incompetent politicians. This is a comfortable illusion supporting a business-as-usual mentality—a mentality that continues to pervade our thinking amid the growing signs of an approaching breakdown in our economic system. Excessive taxation of individuals has robbed us of incentive and made overtime unprofitable. We once produced about 40 percent of the world's steel, we now produce approximately 19 percent.

Let's slice through this rhetoric. The answer to a government that is too big is to stop feeding it. Our government spending has been growing faster than the economy itself. The massive national debt has accumulated as a result of our government's high spending diet. It is certainly time to change the diet and to change it in the proper way. We must first recognize that the problem with our economy is swollen, inefficient government, needless regulation, too much taxation, too much printing-press money. As a country we must now move boldly, decisively, and quickly to control the runaway growth of federal spending, to remove the tax disincentives that are throttling and strangling our economy, and to reform the regulatory web that is smothering it. The United States government is the biggest single debtor in the nation, but it is the image of prudence and parsimony compared to some city governments. And many large corporations, not just Chrysler, are so heavily in debt and illiquid that it probably would not require much of a setback to plunge them into bankruptcy. The level of mortgage debt and consumer debt born by individuals has also reached such high levels that many people nowadays are hardly able to meet their living expenses after they pay their debts. If they lose their jobs, they immediately face a financial crisis.

The message is quite simple: our government is too big and it spends too much money. The decisions that are made in the next few years will set the course of economic and financial events far into the future. Each individual must see that these changes lead not to uncertainty and turmoil but to a new stability based on policies that will optimize and balance real growth, inflation, and employment.

How is any company which operates in a market economy (or any industry of any country for that matter), going to interface with the competition across international boundaries where a very high proportion of world trade is now determined by decisions of government rather than by the decisions of the marketplace? In the long run, even the best managed private companies cannot compete with the tax power of millions of citizens and the credit of their governments. For example, the steel industry by its basic nature is on the leading edge of this issue. The steel industry in this country is not going to disappear; but if it cannot survive as a private enterprise, if it is forced to compete against foreign producers not governed by marketplace disciplines; the steel industry will eventually become an instrument of our government.

President Reagan has stated numerous times his concern about the economy. His interest is real and on target. Inflation in this country is a symptom of economic distress. The truth is that we have inflation because our economy is not productive enough to do all the things that we demand of it. We want it to give us higher incomes, bigger profits, and bigger government programs in the areas where we have a special interest. The federal government must stop spending money we do not have and borrowing to make up the difference. President Reagan says the United States is now facing the worst economic mess since the Great Depression; he also says that we are threatened with an economic calamity of tremendous proportions. These are obviously strong words. Americans should not dismiss them as mere political rhetoric. If one could with reasonable accuracy look into the future, we might see that the United States and the rest of the developed countries are on the way to losing industries such as steel, automobile, railroad equipment, machinery, apparel, shoes, textiles, and appliances. By the end of the century, the Third World will perhaps make 25 percent of the world's manufactured goods. The end of the century is only 19 years away.

What then can we expect of the 1980s? Disappointments—almost certainly in the early years. There are no quick fixes for an inflation that has been with us for over a decade and has been allowed to accelerate sharply in recent years. It will depend on the capacity of the American people for work and willingness to do a job, their energy, and their imagination. Like many of the other issues outstanding in this society, inflation is the buzz word for many of our economic friends who call themselves experts. But how many of these experts have been able to predict with any reasonable accuracy the various peaks and valleys of this country in the last decade. At the present time, this country is in a molded position and a void of elasticity. Yes, it can bounce back. Yes, it can continue to move forward. But if our political process continues to allow our leadership to respond in only political ways, then the American people will be sent adrift on an aged and well-worn ship. This country is somewhat tattered, it is somewhat torn, it has been through many battles. The only course it can take to weather the storms will be by and through the direction of professional leadership. That is the issue, an issue that must be addressed by all men and women. No longer can this society be governed by insecure and unbending forces. The future of America is now in the hands of a few; the future of America should be in the hands of all.

Regulations

Regulations in our society are often regarded as evils which encroach on the rights and freedoms of businesses as well as individuals. The government is seen many times as an all-encompassing big brother that prohibits discretionary choices. In some respects it is ironic that regulation has such a negative image, when in fact the purpose of regulation is to protect the general public. It certainly stands to reason that one cannot strengthen the weak by weakening the strong; you cannot help the wage earner by pulling down the wage payer. You cannot help the poor by destroying the rich, and you cannot help men and women permanently by doing for them what they could and should do for themselves.

The single most important change to our regulatory process should be a switch to a goals-oriented approach. Our government should quit issuing standards on product formulation or engineering design that it often is not particularly qualified to make. Instead government should tell the business community what it wants accomplished, and let business figure out the most effective and most efficient way to reach that objective. At the present time regulation tends to expand in direct proportion to its failures as failure is used to justify the need for a larger budget and additional regulatory powers. It is now imperative that Congress and the President assume the responsibility for preventing the misuse of regulatory powers. The power of the regulatory agencies has grown so much that they have become a fourth branch of government—a branch where the basic checks and balances are lacking. We cannot allow this zeal for regulating almost every aspect of our domestic affairs to spill over into even our international activities. Our newer restrictions based on human rights considerations and antiboycott, antibribery objectives are considered laughable abroad; in fact, many companies are laughing all the way to the bank.

In some respects it seems as though the 1980s are going to be somewhat like the mid-1800s. In that respect one begins to fear one's own government. And this fear is being felt in the boardroom and by stockholders and ordinary working people. Regulatory agencies must begin to view their roles differently. They need to be more sensitive to the broad public interest, to be above petty bureaucratic intrigues, and to be more constructive and less punitive in their enforcement policies. For many years we have been fleecing our golden goose instead of nourishing it. We need to strengthen our parameters and our population against hostile animals on the outer fringes of our fires. We need to mount a concerted campaign to win back the full confidence and support of the American public, of American business. To abandon this direction would be to abandon a commitment to a freedom that began over 200 years ago.

It is not intended to suggest that all regulations are bad or that all regulations are good. Certainly sometimes agencies outlive their usefulness. Sometimes changed circumstances render agencies obsolete, sometimes they lose sight of their mission and their constituencies and devote their efforts to empire building and self-perpetuation. And sometimes they get so bogged down with caseload they forget why they're there in the first place. Much of our regulatory legislation was intended to provide the public and especially consumers with protection against perceived ills. In many instances we must reassess not only the efficiency of that protection, but also whether the economic, legal, and social burdens of maintaining this legislative insurance are worth such protection. All regulation is costly, not only because it is payed for by taxation, but also because it interferes with market forces, increases the size and complexity of government, and favors one group of people in our society over another.

Today's current reaction against regulation is based on a number of concerns. For example, when regulation is discussed by both business leaders as well as politicians, there seems to be an unstated assumption that regulation is the antithesis of free enterprise. It should be stated here that ill-conceived regulation can severely frustrate the advantages and efficiencies of a free-market economy. One should not assume that the simple removal of regulatory statutes will result in increased competition. If deregulation is based on the assumption that competition will control the market, we must be sure that a high degree of competition will in fact exist when regulatory controls are removed.

Today, the economy of the United States is under severe strain. Its daily headlines read like the hospital chart of a very sick patient, all vital signs are moving in the wrong direction. What should be of concern to every American is the variances of range of forces pitted against the survival of the patient. These forces come in the guises of social restructuring, regulatory control, political reform, and just plain hostility. Regulation has its place. But it is obvious that the burden of regulation on today's economy and today's business population is excessive. Perhaps this regulatory overprotection is an omen that our society will be wallowing in quicksand with the outstretched branch of regulation as its only means of support. American business no longer needs that kind of support; its survival cannot be predicated on an improper foundation, weak from history and unable to strategically place itself. American business can only survive with strength and forward planning. The question then is will it be able to exchange the tattered uniform of yesterday for the sensibility and forward thinking needed for tomorrow?

Women and minorities

Rationale for affirmative action as it began a number of years ago was best stated by the late President Lyndon Johnson when he said that, "to be black in a white society is not to stand on level and equal ground." While the races may stand side by side, whites stand on history's mountain and blacks stand in history's hollow. Substitute "women" or "minorities" for "blacks," and the same situation holds true. Until this country overcomes unequal history, we cannot overcome unequal opportunity. It's time to get down to the business of trying to stand black and white (and women and minorities) on level ground. In specific areas we must set new goals and new objectives and new standards.

The long-term health of this economy and of the private sector depends on whether it comes to make maximum creative use of *all* the human resources at its disposal. It wasn't until the South was forced to abandon segregation that is suddenly blossomed into economic growth patterns the rest of the nation envies. As industry lowered discriminatory barriers against other ethnic minorities, it profited from their skills and their drive to succeed. The private sector cannot survive without an infusion of new blood, without tapping the talents of those it has neglected in the past. Some companies have learned to recruit at black campuses, to hire and train blacks, to promote black employees to managerial ranks, and they have undoubtedly profited from it. Black people and women have suffered discrimination in the past. They still suffer from the effects of past discrimination combined with continuing discrimination based on negative stereotypes and irrational prejudices. A case for affirmative action does not rest on the few who have made it, but on the many who have not. Blacks and women as a group remain disproportionately disadvantaged, denied equal social and economic opportunities.

The civil rights laws, more than most, have been and continue to be indifferently enforced and somewhat largely ignored. The new activist enforcement policies are thus to be applauded. The Julian Bonds are the indirect forces that continue to assist and make new inroads for women and blacks. The 1980s will see a pressing ahead in an accelerated posture on affirmative action. It will be made a top-level priority for American business. And the Equal Rights Amendment is the bottom-line for all working women. Remember that there is only one way to measure the success, and that's by the numbers.

In time, perhaps, the attitudes that serve as roadblocks for both minorities and women will go away. What it takes is a firm commitment on the part of every business leader in a corporate setting to try to understand each other. Peter Drucker, the noted economist and author, suggested that the only things that evolve by themselves in a business setting are disorder, friction, and malperformance. It is people who move the company toward its goals. In the last couple of years, the Weber case removed a major question mark hanging over affirmative action programs in employment. Recently the Bakke rule, although vague, did affirm the court's long-standing commitment to affirmative action that redresses past discrimination. Whether it was important because it extended the affirmative action remedy to societal discrimination without regard to whether the specific employer had a history of past discrimination or not. The problems ahead are formidable. Yet all too often these problems are used as a smokescreen to hide the backsliding on affirmative action and the timidity of public officials who refuse to make hard but fair choices in allocating resources. Minorities, women, black and white, call it what you may, this country's foundation was built on equality. Certainly equality has not reigned supreme these many years. The qualifications of women, of minorities, are certainly acceptable in today's world. Women and minorities everywhere should have an equal voice, an equal opportunity. Unfortunately, in this decade, total equality can only come about and will only happen through pressure, not by fairness and the need to do what is right.

Inflation

The business corporation of the 1980s will be as different from that of the 70s as the corporation of the 40s was from that of the 20s. The experience will not be as wrenching as it was 30 to 40 years ago when business was dragged protesting all the way into the New Deal era. By the end of this decade, many of our business families will be so diversified as to be virtually unrecognizable to someone who has not followed them closely. And why is this happening? Simply, inflation. Inflation is impacting the capital market; inflation is driving up the level of interest rates; inflation is weakening the willingness of many people to save for the future; inflation has a corrosive effect; inflation is discouraging capital investment and hampering the improvement of productivity; inflation, not design, will erode away much of the strength of American business. Perhaps this won't happen; perhaps American business can be a strong force in our society and the free world. Perhaps we can overcome the terrible pressures of inflation. Or perhaps we will be completely knuckled under to big government by 1989 as our British friends and others are; perhaps everyone will be wearing the golden handcuffs in Washington.

If this decade is going to be one of strength and of forward movement, then how can we cure inflation? A combination of tax limitation and spending limitation at the federal government level is certainly an answer to be reckoned with. To prevent the value of our money from being diluted, we must put a limit on the authority of the Congress to spend. If government continues to expand its influence over the lives of its citizens as it has for the last 40 or more years, future generations will be denied that opportunity for incentive, for high productivity, for personal choice of work, of education, literature, and beliefs. As our government reaches deeper into the lives of each of us, our economic freedom will become diminished, and our personal and political freedoms will slowly slip away. How can we solve this problem? Only people can solve and stop inflation. To be effective in curbing inflation, we should understand the causes of inflation. We should redirect our efforts from finding hedges against inflation to taking the necessary individual and societal actions to fight inflation. We should recognize that trying to profit from inflation is a dangerous strategy because by taking such actions we add fuel to an already overheated economy. And many of the vehicles being used to gain from inflation, such as silver, art and stamps, may be reaching their peak prices.

American business is clearly a loser in several ways. Because most people think higher prices *are* inflation, business is the constant bearer of the bad news as prices are pushed up by inflation. Because of the unpredictable nature of inflation and government antiinflationary actions, American business does not know how to make long-term decisions on prices, wages, inventories, and future capital investments. Inflation is a divisive element in our society, a slowly working cancer that is destructive to our basic values. Inflation spreads doubt about the free enterprise system itself, and more and more people feel that they are constantly having to work harder and harder just to maintain their present standard of living. This general frustration and resentment will have serious social consequences in the future.

The federal government, since it is the only one that can legally print money, is responsible for starting inflation. The action by the Federal Reserve Board and system creates money and controls the total money supply and interest rates. If the federal government does not cover the deficit by creating new money, the Treasury has to sell bonds that are paid out of private savings. But when did inflation begin? Many economists pinpoint a time somewhere around the mid-1960s. In the 1960s we had Vietnam and many social programs. During that time we decided we would pay some of the cost later, and that should have been an important signal that we were making a mistake. If those actions were so important to our society, why didn't we pay for them at that time? Inflation, unfortunately, is going to get worse and perhaps even beyond our control. At least it will if we do not take the right steps and take the right steps now. Since our government has caused the problem, it will have to do the most to solve it. We are going to have to take a lot of discipline from our society to control government budget deficits and to limit the money supply growth. The overwhelming passage of Proposition 13 in California was a vote by people against inflation, not against local government. They knew that the high property taxes were caused by an increased value of property due to inflation.

Unfortunately, our government as a whole still refuses to come to grips with the core issue of the problem—and that is government spending. More and more paper money is printed to pay the bills, and the federal debt goes up and up and up and up. It now stands at approximately $800+ billion, and the annual interest alone is over $75 billion. Surprising to many, the biggest losers have been the rich who got caught at the beginning of this decade with their assets in stocks, bonds, and other sorts of long-term loans such as mortgages. But regardless of whoever gets hurt, inflation destroys savings, it wrecks pensions and retirement incomes, and it consumes the capital needed to improve jobs and increase living standards. Inflation lets the strong exploit the weak. Accounting becomes deceptive, profits become illusory, and business cycles fluctuate even more widely.

Today, respect for our government decreases further as we see federal officials jawboning others such as business, labor, and hospitals. Inflation hits many of the poor and elderly especially hard, and this breeds discontent. It continues to create bitterness between economic classes, as the poor perceive their helplessness and lack of sophistication in developing hedges against or profiting from inflation. Inflation exists today because the politicians to whom we have given responsibility to guard the value of our currency have had neither the courage nor the will to do it. I believe that most Americans still value individual liberty and freedom even though they may not understand the connection between individual freedom and free enterprise. It is the responsibility of this country's business leaders to explain to them how the two are inseparable. If we lose one, we lose them both.

Only by keeping free enterprise alive and well and thriving in America can we also keep freedom alive and well. The question still remaining is will America's third century be recessional? It certainly will not if we take the right road now. But can we find the right road, can we cut through the rhetoric and determine the proper path? Unless we attack directly the basic cause of inflation, which is government deficits and fiscal policies, guidelines certainly will not help. Guidelines deal with effects, not causes. Guidelines are like a movable finish line. To be realistic, they must be extended continually to accommodate rising inflation.

For example, social security costs cannot be ignored any longer. Forecasts for the future solvency of the plan are not encouraging, and social security may not survive. Attempts to alleviate the problem through increases in payroll taxes and business contributions are only going to be counterproductive. The purchasing power of the consuming public is already strained, and there have to be better solutions.

Inflation is so incredibly damaging that we as a society cannot simply continue to live with it. Perhaps credit allocation could well be one of the sparks to set off the blaze. Inflation has encouraged spending beyond our means. Our spending and borrowing has accelerated as we have tried to put our declining dollars into property that will retain or gain in value.

Freedom, if you will, is a tender plant. It is rare, hard to start, difficult to cultivate, and needs constant attention or else it dies easily. And what of America, are we still free? Yes, but not as free as last year, and considerably less free than 10 years ago, and a great deal less free than 40 years ago. Freedom, like clean air, is hardly noticed as it is fading until suddenly one day it is gone. And it may be too late to get it back. Inflation is putting a stranglehold on our freedom, on our ability to move, to make decisions, to be innovative and creative. Inflation can be controlled by people, but only people who are strong leaders and who are not in it for themselves. If we can get over the inflation hurdle, then American business in the 1980s will regain much of its former luster. It will be able to compete better in world markets, and it can spend more time developing the goods and services that will better meet people's needs. It can realistically work toward energy requirements without the specter of OPEC's latest price increases. The American businessman and woman and the corporation are the country's hope for the future.

Government

The demand of this country throughout the 1980's will not be for smaller government or bigger government but for better government. Many critics today say that government is always bad and that spending for basic social problems is the root of our economic evils. The task of leadership in the 1980s will be not to parade scapegoats or to seek refuge in reaction as we have so often in the past, but to match our power to the possibilities of progress. Hard decisions are going to have to be made because decisions and investments in this decade and the 1990s will determine the character and path that this society and American business will take into the 21st century. Managers of this decade and the 1990s will have to be more sensitive to the corporate social responsibilities by acting in the larger interest of society. The managers of today and tomorrow, especially tomorrow, will have to possess great political sophistication since governments everywhere, unfortunately, will continue their attempts to be even more pervasive forces in the economic life of people. Managers will have to become students of public affairs.

The many failures of American government and society in recent times have indicated the traditional discontent of intellectuals. On all levels of our society, not only among the educated, elite, or the excluded minorities, one finds a growing belief that our institutions are not only flawed but also too costly to repair. Unfortunately, many have or are beginning to view our society as a failed society; they think it is time for everyone to get their own while the getting is good. If there is to be a turnaround in this kind of feeling, then the successors in management of American business must be future-oriented, must be aware of the forces that work around them internationally as well as domestically, and must be able to anticipate the direction of change, if not the details of change itself. The top managers of this decade are with us now or soon to be joining us. They are the best and the brightest of the baby-boom of the post-World War II era, and there are lots of them. Competition for management posts by these men and women now in their 30s and 40s is going to be frightful in the next decade. Unfortunately, it is small wonder that well-meaning business people and others now throw up their hands in disgust. We do not just have the failure of government to come to grips with or the problems of the economy that irritate the public, it's government regulation, it's government insecurity, it's government's misdirected direction.

An example of government and its misdirection is the explosion in the pages of the *Federal Register* from 1970 to 1980; it went from 20,032 pages to 87,012 pages, reflecting the exponential growth of the federal bureaucracy's control of our lives. Another example is a statute called the Employee Retirement Income Security Act, commonly known as ERISA. It started with excellent intentions but has become encrusted with wasteful regulations, filings, and reports that do not result in one additional dollar of retirement benefits for most employees, but do impose millions of dollars of nonproductive costs on employers. The original statute was 247 pages; the conference committee report was 140 pages. The act has been amended regularly; the text of the latest amendment covers 103 pages. Regulations under the act were issued by the Departments of Labor and Treasury. There is now sufficient material to fill 6,000 pages in a five-volume, loose-leaf service published by Commerce Clearing House. Under the present law many large corporations must file an excess of 4,000 pages annually to comply with ERISA reporting requirements.

We should recognize that a civil servant is as capable of abusing authority as any other human being. Government can abuse, government has abused. President Reagan has indicated by his initial actions that he intends to move decisively to cut back on the bureaucracy in Washington. Reagan fully recognizes that this country has a big problem and that the government is ineffective, expensive, counterproductive, and unresponsive. Government is self-bloating, and therefore, government cannot find the means by which it can reduce itself. What we should do is to put our glasses aside and look at this country straight on; let some of our natural American confidence and realistic confidence come back, not necessarily based only on the hopes all Americans share for Reagan's administration but based more importantly on the underlying vigor of this country. We made it through the 10 bitter years of Vietnam and Watergate—crises that tested the United States constitution. We moved forward, sometimes under decent presidents, sometimes under mediocre presidents and leadership. Perhaps Americans are underestimating the strength of this country and what it is working from. Not to be optimistic, but what we need to do today and tomorrow is to renew ourselves. We have new faces in the high office, new faces for the big jobs in Washington, new mayors, new governors, new representatives, new senators. This country can move forward, but it can only move forward if we are realistic. We can only move forward if there is a passion for justice, if there is a concern for order and not the ability to do mischief.

Government is by the people and for the people. We are government. We elect our leadership, and we supposedly give them direction. But that is not the way it has worked. We have elected, and they have gone forward with or without our direction. They have gone forward without our direction because we have not given it to them—we have lost interest. We have not given our support after election day to those who lead this country. Yes, government has not done it, but neither have we.

Multinationals

There have been enumerable studies undertaken on the impact of transnational corporations on host countries. Certainly the press many times has had the world believing that TNC's make decisions that are totally contrary to legislation. But in many, many circles and at many times this has proved otherwise. The bottomline certainly suggests that when a multinational company operates in a particular country, it tends to raise the standard of living and increase the wealth of that country.

For representatives of transnationals, their interests in their long-term peace and well-being suggest that they must begin to stand up and be counted on the issues of the day. They must join in the decision making process at the national level. Certainly too much is at stake to remain aloof. They have to begin to inform others and to broaden the constituency for the transnational viewpoint. As each new country declares its independence, it always seems that its list of priorities includes a new flag and a national airline. The TNCs have set themselves up in a commericial relationship, not only with existing nations, but also with emerging countries. The impact a TNC has on a developing or newly industrialized nation is quite different than the impact it has on a so-called country. Certainly the TNC does not have powers beyond the control of sovereign governments, and it certainly is not completely free to do as it will. Because this planet becomes more and more crowded and smaller with each passing day, the impact of the TNC on a host country is both important and extremely beneficial.

The 1980s will find industrial nations fostering considerably freer trade with the developing nations. Clearly, their future growth and living standards depend upon their ability to export manufactured goods to the developed world. What would be truly alarming in this decade is a growing strength of protectionist sentiment. The decibel level of disputes and strong-arm rhetoric could rise rapidly. Governments are and will be concerned more about trade imbalances than unemployment in industries affected by foreign competition. But as the world becomes more and more nationalistically fragmented, a connecting link of mutual interests is going to be essential for peace and prosperity. The TNC will be that link. The TNC should be proud of its role and not beat its breast. In fact, it should recognize that it has as great a stake in the welfares of the people as any government.

Unions

This decade will highlight this country's expression of a desire for change. Union chieftains are now discussing regrouping and unification. Employees want a bigger say in company actions affecting their particular futures. Organized labor at least early in this decade, will not be getting tough with the Reagan administration. Clearly the labor movement cannot be bullish about itself; now there is an unfriendly Senate, a less sympathetic House, and an unobligated Reagan administration. Labor in the 1980s no longer can indulge itself in featherbedding or archaic make-work practices. There is no more brotherhood of locomotive firemen; there is no more dead horse setting the Bible in the back shop at a newspaper just to put in hours. Union laborers do cling to the Davis Bacon Law, which requires federal contractors to pay prevailing union wages so as to make it easier for such contractors to deal with unions.

But let's not kid ourselves, there will be a labor movement. There is talk about social concepts and sharing in management decisions. That adversary relationship must continue to keep balance. With fringe benefits at about the 40 percent level and organized labor's considerable concern over keeping the status quo, union management will continue to live on and play a vital role in American business.

As the makeup of employees shifts from blue-collar to service and white-collar, unions will find many more potential clients. Unless American business changes its management style, its communication efforts, etc., the savvy union organizing team should have a heyday in its ability and opportunity to organize these new categories of employees.

Labor just won't fight to hold on to what it has. We'll see demands for more time off and for extensive protection against plant closings in the form of earlier pensions and crippling, long, preclosing-notice periods. Labor heretofore has proven very poor at organizing the unorganized, and for the first time it has reached the sorry state of losing more elections than it wins. Thus, American business will see more demands for neutrality, the hard-to-swallow practice in which management agrees not to resist attempts to organize its production workers. Unions will increasingly work to conserve what they have. Unions have long called for the right to have a voice in how the hundreds of billions of dollars in pension plans are administered, and in time during this decade they will have that right. The 1980s may be a turning point for the labor movement. Labor during this period will sputter but have successes. The American labor movement will go into a semipermanent decline or, at least, experience a substantial loss in prestige and power. Its salvation will be in the white-collar ranks because unless American business learns how to clearly communicate, clearly motivate, and clearly have the sensitivity to deal with its office and professional ranks, then the organizer pounding on the front door will receive if not a welcome, at least a handshake wrapped in curiosity.

America

Walter Lippman once reminded us, "You took the good things for granted, now you must earn them again. For every night that you cherish, you have a duty which you must fulfill; for every hope that you entertain, you have a task that you must perform; for every good that you wish to preserve, you will have to sacrifice your comfort and your ease. There is nothing for nothing any longer." The challenges for this country in the 1980s are going to be formidable, but it goes without saying that there is a new spirit and unity in this country for this decade. And, with confidence and hope, the Reagan administration and its new vision will carry this country forward.

The 20th century has been called the American century. We, as a country, have had considerable self-examination. The Vietnam and Watergate experiences, as well as present rising energy prices, and our dependence on foreign oil, have continued to badger us. Americans are beginning to suggest that perhaps we don't deserve our successes of the past and that we haven't as a society properly planned and allowed ourselves to be prepared for those issues. America the Beautiful has become America the Apologetic; but America is a land of the handicapped, the minority who are not white, and the majority who are women, and all have suffered injustice even with the legal support of equal pay and equal opportunity.

The decade of the 1980s will certainly be a decade of doubt and indecision, but in between the clouds of blight and insecurity will be the shining bright rays of promise and hope. There is no doubt that as a world we have the resources, technology, management know-how, and capital to resume the upward climb. The question really is, can we get our act together efficiently and fast enough to make those necessary adjustments.

There are many questions that confront this nation. How can we reclaim our cities? Can we break the back of inflation? Will there be continuing decline in our rate of productivity improvement? How can we lessen our dependence on foreign oil? What about the problems of the aged? Can our social security system become solvent? How do we provide our American workers with jobs that are rewarding not only financially but psychologically as well? How do we restore confidence in business?

These are never easy questions because the United States is a very difficult country today, more difficult than at any other period in its short history. We have a great responsibility to free societies everywhere since much of the world still looks at our nation for leadership.

Yes, the United States economy is still the world's most productive. But this fact is by no means a smug call for inaction. Mr. John K. Collings, Jr., vice chairman of The Coca-Cola Company, summarizes the fate of America when he suggests that:

"The stamp, 'Made in America,' no longer identifies those products bought in and outside of this country. Our angel at the top of the tree has dimmed its light. This country is no longer in a prosperity position of being competitive. The leadership of American business must pull tightly on the reins to secure a sound direction for the future. The insecurity that entraps the CEOs and other leaders of American business must be swept aside. America is beautiful, America can be successful once again. But the blinders that have discouraged its growth and forward thrust must be removed so that prosperity and a fine competitive edge can once again be part of this great country's calling card. It is time to revitalize American business."

Energy

The decade of the 1960s was a time for new freedoms and environmental awareness. The decade of the 1970s was one of changing values, mistrust, and everyone for him/herself. The 1980s are going to be years of coming to grips with reality once more. The energy crisis today is real, it is worldwide, it is a clear and present danger to our nation. But the underlying cause of the energy crisis, the energy problem, the energy challenge, is the same as it has been for many years. That is, our massive, dangerous, growing dependence on oil and particularly our excessive dependence on imported oil.

The energy future is bleak and is likely to grow bleaker during this decade. The widespread fantasy that this country contains enormous proven reserves of oil which are hidden and unreported is sometimes difficult to explain. In reality, this country is not energy-poor, it does have huge energy resources if we but have the determination to develop them and willingness to pay for their cost. For example, there is sufficient domestic uranium to fuel existing and planned nuclear reactors throughout their 40-year life span. The shale oil contained in the shale beds of the Rocky Mountains far exceeds the crude oil resources of all the Arab nations in the Middle East. This country has nearly one-third of the world's known coal. Coal enough not to last for years but for centuries.

The Congress is twisted and pulled in every direction by hundreds of well-financed and powerful special interest groups. In the last election which brought President Reagan to the forefront, we saw every extreme position defended to the last vote, almost to the last breath, by one unyielding group or another. Yes, our energy problem is serious, and it is getting worse. We are wasting too much energy; we are buying far too much oil from foreign countries; and we are not producing enough oil, gas, or coal in this country. The self-appointed leaders are using the nuclear energy issue as a vehicle to promote social, political, and economic change in this country. Fingerpointing and blame placing at this stage are clearly counterproductive. A prerequisite for an effective national energy program is to recognize that we are all to blame to one degree or another; the government for failing to recognize the long-term nature of the supply problem and for not launching a program of positive action, the public for ignoring the problem, and our politicians for not developing a dialogue with their constituencies on the real issues involved.

Today nothing is more critical to our society than the availability of an adequate energy supply. But that does not necessarily mean adequate oil. The dilemma is quite clear: we must make greater use of coal and nuclear power with the technologies available today, or alternatively we face reduced economic growth and rising levels of unemployment. Coal perhaps is the logical candidate to meet the immediate needs. Although coal accounts for 90 percent of the nation's conventional energy reserves, it supplies less than 20 percent of our energy needs. And what about nuclear power; is it safe? It certainly involves some risk, but we know of no other high-technology industry which can point to the most serious accident in its history and say truthfully that no one was killed or injured. Nuclear power growth in the United States has been stopped dead because of the Three Mile Island accident. Other countries, however, with little oil or coal resources, are going ahead with their nuclear development programs. France expects to be generating one half of its electricity from nuclear resources by 1985. In all of the debate that has swirled around nuclear power in recent days, the bottomline has to be that if we want to keep the lights on, we have to move forward in the use of nuclear power. Already nuclear power provides about 13 percent of America's electricity, with the nuclear portion being as high as 50 percent in a number of areas. It is obvious from many studies that the management of nuclear reactors has been sharply upgraded because of the Three Mile Island accident. No one should forget the safety record of the industry, before and since Three Mile Island. It is better than the record of any other energy-related industry or, as a matter of fact, of any other industry period. This country is faced with gigantic problems that require understanding and a balancing of pros and cons, of benefits and risks. Energy as one significant element in this country's menagerie of problems is the lifeblood of our economic system. However, another possibility for new energy sources is solar energy. Solar energy at the present time seems certainly very useful for select purposes, such as the initial investment to heat water. It is marginal yet fairly economical for heating homes. But insofar as large scale use, for example electric-power purposes, it still seems somewhat out of reach. Most of this country still fails to recognize that solar power's greatest proven attribute is for comfort heating, and that means saving other resources, mostly oil and natural gas.

During the past 20 years we have had no energy policy of any depth or substance. The lack of a well-defined energy policy has greatly contributed in large measure to our growing dependence on foreign oil. In 1955 Americans consumed somewhat less than 9 million barrels of oil per day, but in the late 70s, consumption had grown to nearly 19 million barrels per day. The energy problem is not just a question of comfort or maintaining what is called the quality of life; it is a more important question, an issue of economic and political independence, of maintaining freedom for our children and our grandchildren.

It is our great fortune to be one of the richest energy nation's in the world. Yet judging by our current economic conditions, who would know that. Shortages of gasoline and fuel are widely feared. But it is not fair to say that energy has been ignored over the years. President Carter, for example, proposed several energy programs, and the Democratic Congress acted on hundreds of energy bills in the last six years. Some things have been done. But what has been done is the impeding of production and curtailing of consumption. The government acted on the principle that the way to deal with energy was to do away with it. The question now comes to mind whether we really need more energy. Is this what we need to consider when we think about our children?

Today we face a world crisis of vaster dimensions than Churchill described a half century ago when he talked about world crisis, and the crisis today is made more ominous by the problems of oil. The labor force in the year 2000 (already born) will be one-third larger than at present, and those are your children and grandchildren we are addressing.

In wrestling with the issue of energy, the auto industry as a principle industry will have a major contribution to make. The role of the government will be to set the overall context and direction of national energy policy and to provide a reliable climate for industry to operate. The car industry, for its own sake if it is going to have adequate markets in the future, will have to step up the drive to increase energy efficiency, to reassess the energy inputs that go into the auto manufacturing process, and to look forward to the new transport fuels that will have to be developed, such as coal, synthetics, electricity, etc. By 1990 this country will have to manage a transition to a new energy supply structure or we will face a serious energy crisis accompanied by severe economic recession. Slow down is certainly not a viable way to deal with the energy problem; it only postpones the situation and in the long term makes it worse. There is a critical role for each individual to play. It is not a matter of good intentions but of technology, organizational structure, and experience. The energy problem is not a cause for embarrassment, and perhaps not even long-term concern, if we act promptly to develop a coordinated national energy policy. As a nation, we have shown repeatedly that we can rise to the challenge. There isn't a shortage of fuels provided everyone is willing to pay enough to turn motion into concentrated forms of energy.

But if you look at the statistics around us, for example 92 percent of all the energy consumed in New York State comes from out of state; oil accounts for two thirds of New York State's total energy consumption compared to less than half of the nation's; approximately 90 percent of New York State's oil is imported making it the largest consumer of OPEC oil in the United States; 90 percent of New York State's natural gas originates from Louisiana; and nearly all of New York State's coal comes from the Appalachian region. This decade must be one in which we again find our bearing on energy. Straightening out this country's energy problems won't be easy; it's going to be a big job. But we have the expertise and the people, and we can do that job. This is a country that has a national addiction to waste and overconsumption, and unfortunately but perhaps quite timely, the proper priority and attention is now being given to this addiction. America is about to enter a new era of productivity, for its entire industrial complex will not be restricted to just energy but will be extended to all areas which comprise our economy. During this era we will face facts. There is simply not enough oil available in the world to meet all of the demands of all the people in all the nations on earth. Yes, potentially this country does have ample supply, but in reality we are not prepared or able to extract and to make use of all that potential. We will need to control our demands, to cut back on the waste of energy, and to develop our own sources of energy to replace foreign imports so that we can better control our own destiny. The energy issue is serious, critical, and can in the long term deal a strategic and damaging blow to America. Like this country's other issues, again the senility of insecurity will continue to pull down the past heroics of America. Until strong leadership is justified and supported can issues like energy be handled properly with long-term, positive results.

The 1980s

We can characterize the 1980's as a dangerous decade for every American because whatever our political persuasion, we will all lose if this backward journey to past benign neglect and injustice is accomplished. We can all tell something is wrong in America when we hear the question does God hear our prayers or when the Ku Klux Klan openly solicits an invitation to march in an inaugural parade in full regalia. An unknown writer once said, "It was not until I went into the heartlands of America and into her churches and met the American people that I discovered what it is that makes America great. America is great because America is good, and if America ever ceases to be good, America will cease to be great." I think we all took too many things for granted, certainly the good things. Now we must run them all back again. For every right that we cherish we have a duty which we must fulfill; for every good which we wish to preserve, we will have to sacrifice our comfort and our ease. We get nothing for nothing. In the 1980s the American economic system, like our political system, will continue to be untidy. It will offend those people who love tidy, predictable societies. But there is not going to be any going back to the simpler times of the one-room schoolhouse. Those times certainly were enjoyable, but as a society we must be addicted to the future. With the support of the American people, government in recent decades has helped to dismantle racial barriers. But in the 1980's because of so many decisions regarding priorities, the question still remains as to whether we can provide for the jobless and retired, feed the hungry, protect consumers, insure bargaining rights for workers, and still continue to preserve our national heritage.

We will continue to have inflation. We as a society have an inflationary mentality. For the past 20 years, this country has been borrowing against its national insurance policy. We have not been working to build our values. In the great comfort of our extraordinary affluence, we have come to believe that the lives of men and women are largely cost free. We have paid little attention to the unpleasant fact that great civilizations have periods of ascendency and also periods of decline. It goes without saying that this country is on the threshold of an exciting decade. Electronic technology is our bridge to the future. But the issues abound and are plentiful, issues that must be attacked for simplicity and correction. This country has enormous recuperative powers. Our political institutions are resilient and flexible. Our bookshelves today are piled high with books warning us that the pace of change has become too much for human beings to tolerate. It is not just risk that people fear, but the future itself. We must never accept a permanent group of unemployed Americans any longer. Women and blacks need a chance. Business and labor need to be ever increasingly supportive. Government needs to stop its excessive growth and to control its spending habits. Many of the problems that we will face in the 1980s will be most amenable to small-scale, fine-grain solutions. This country has made mistakes, and it will make more. Some of them will be moral mistakes. But no great power in history has been so consistently selfless in its foreign policy. This fact should be a matter of national pride. We must act today in order to preserve tomorrow. All Americans must bear the burden.

"It was a bright, cold day in April and the clocks were striking thirteen." That is the opening sentence of George Orwell's novel *1984*. In the book Orwell made 137 predictions, and so far over 100 of his visions have become reality in the incredibly short span of just three decades. The 1980s are not hard to predict. The issues are basic, and the answers are equally simple. It will be a frustrating time because we are in a frustrating society. It is tragic that many of our leaders today feel they must mortgage the future to become either elected or maintain their status quo. The American dream became a reality because of the combination of personal liberty, free enterprise, and integrity. This country, the United States of America, is the only nation on earth deliberately created not on the basis of geography or tribal allegiances but on behalf of an *idea*. The idea was liberty. Our leaders come from the people. In the 1980s, no one should doubt America's continued greatness. America, American business, the people, have overcome every obstacle. America and American business put a man on the moon in the 60s. America and American business developed a destructive power of nuclear energy to end a world war. America and American business launched the clipper ships to trade anywhere in the world. America and American business are a successful combination in center court. For those in this book who took time to express their thoughts and to give further direction for this country and for those who helped behind the scenes, the 1980s will be the next important step forward.

Notes

Chapter 1

1. "How to Halt Excessive Government Regulation," *Nation's Business*, March 1976, p. 47.
2. Interview with Julian Bond. All quotations hereafter, unless footnoted and otherwise indicated, are derived from personal interviews.
3. Elliott Levitas, "Can Congress Control the Regulators?" *Industry Week*, March 29, 1976, p. 20.
4. I. W. Abel, speech at American Medical Association Conference, New York City, 1977.
5. Edmund G. Brown, Jr., speech.
6. "Providing Facts So Regulation Won't Read Like Fiction," *Industry Week*, February 9, 1976, p. 42.
7. *Congressional Record*, vol. 123, no. 12, January 24, 1977, p. 27.
8. Thornton Bradshaw, speech at University of Southern California Commerce Association dinner, May 5, 1976.
9. Ibid.
10. Ibid.

Chapter 2

1. Remarks by former Secretary of Commerce Juanita Kreps at the Fourth Annual International Trade Conference of the Southeast, Dallas, Texas, May 24, 1977.

2. Irving Shapiro, speech.

3. Ibid.

4. Elliott Richardson, speech.

Chapter 3

1. For a brief overview of trends in the development of multinational corporations, see Peter C. Vale, *The Multinational Corporation: An Introduction,* Braamfontein: South African Institute of International Affairs, 1974, pp. 2–4. For a much more detailed account, see two books by Mira Wilkins. *The Emergence of Multinational Enterprise* (Cambridge, Mass.: Harvard University Press, 1970) deals with MNC developments up to World War I. *The Maturing of Multinational Enterprise*, Harvard Studies in Business History, no. 27 (Cambridge, Mass.: 1974) completes the survey through 1970.

2. Jacques C. Maisonrouge, "The Mythology of Multinationalism," *Columbia Journal of World Business*, Spring 1974, p. 8. Maisonrouge feels that multinational corporations must meet other criteria as well. These include operation in countries that have attained varying degrees of economic development, involvement of host country nationals in the management of local operations, multinational stock ownership, and multinational management of corporate operations.

3. Ibid.

4. Ibid.

5. Ibid. Also see the discussion of Vernon's concept by Vale, *The Multinational Corporation*, p. 1.

6. Ibid.

7. Ibid.

8. Henry A. Kissinger, U.S. Department of State, PR 408, p. 12.

9. Ibid, pp. 12–13.

10. Rawleigh Warner, Jr., "A Call to Reason," Business Keynote Address to the 61st Annual Convention of the National Foreign Trade Council, New York, N.Y., November 18, 1974.

11. Remarks by Former Secretary of Commerce Juanita Kreps, at the Fourth Annual International Trade Conference of the Southwest, Dallas, Texas, May 24, 1977.

12. Wilkins, *The Maturing of Multinational Enterprise.* See the chapter on "The Environment for Multinational Business," pp. 327ff.

13. The possibilities for corruption in situations involving close government-business collaboration are not difficult to divine. For an assessment of such developments in Japan, the country Young selects as an example of the collaboration he envisions, see William Safire, "Remember Japan, Inc.," *The New York Times,* August 9, 1976.

14. Kissinger, U.S. Department of State, PR #408, p. 11.

15. Ibid., p. 13.

16. Ibid., p. 12.

17. Ibid., p. 7.

18. Ibid., p. 9.

19. Ibid., p. 6.

20. It should not be inferred from the discussion that the voluntary codes and guidelines developed thus far are wholly without their defects. See, for example, "MN Firms Unhappy with 'Unbalanced' UN Report," *Industry Week*, July 8, 1974, pp. 18ff. This article cites criticism of the UN report on the grounds that it dwells overmuch on the activities of multinational corporations in the underdeveloped world.

Chapter 4

1. "Americans Change," February 20, 1978, p.44.

2. Ibid.

3. Ibid.

4. Gerald R. Ford, speech, Invest in America luncheon, Washington, D.C., May 24, 1977.

5. I.W. Abel, speech, AMA Conference, New York City, 1977.

6. For a discussion of changing values on the part of management level personnel, see "How Men Are Changing?" *Newsweek*, January 16, 1978, p. 52.

Chapter 5

1. Even as we begin this effort to define the "energy problem", some preliminary definition of basic terms is needed. "Energy" is defined as the force, power, drive, etc., that makes machines operate and that raises or lowers temperature in buildings. Energy resources are the natural elements (e.g.,

petroleum products) that generate these forces, powers, and drives.

2. Remarks by former Representative Thomas Ashley, *Congressional Record,* August 1, 1977, p. H8173.

3. Representative Robert Anderson, *Congressional Record,* August 1, 1977 p. H8174.

4. "The fundamental problem for U.S. energy policy is the insecurity of its oil supply." So begins the report of the Ad Hoc Committee on Energy, U.S. House of Representatives, on the National Energy Act, July 27, 1977, vol. 1, p. 5. I have attempted to expand on this summary statement of the House formulation by reference to some of the other factors (e.g., environmental concerns, alternate energy sources) that I feel are also fundamental to the energy problem. For a journalistic summary of the problem that gives considerable attention to the whole problem of cost, see William Greider and J.P. Smith, "Fuels Crisis, a Matter of Perception," *The Washington Post,* July 24, 1977, p. 1. For a case study that highlights some of the social costs and benefits associated with exploitation of one of this country's more plentiful sources of energy, namely coal, see Paul Edwards, "Strip Mining Brings Prosperity Woes," *Washington Post,* July 31, 1977, p. 1. Also see Michael Shultz, "Mine Drainage Makes Potomac Suffer Greatly," *Baltimore Evening Sun,* August 9, 1977, p. B1.

5. In the remainder of this discussion, the term *energy problem* will refer to the overall formulation which we have suggested in the opening section. Such terms as *energy issues* or *questions related to energy* will refer to specific aspects of the overall problem.

6. For an overview of these enactments, see David E. Gushee and Frances A. Gulick, "Moral Equivalent of War," *Congressional Research Service Bulletin,* 95th Congress, Issue no. 2, July 1977, p. 2.

7. *The Congressional Quarterly Weekly Report* is a highly useful source of detailed yet readable information about activities underway in Congress. For material on the Carter energy plan, see the *Weekly Reports* for April 23, 1977, and May 5, 1977.

8. Rawleigh Warner, Jr., "A Call to Reason," business keynote address to the 61st annual convention of

the National Foreign Trade Council, New York, N.Y., November 18, 1974.

9. Ibid.

10. The 50 percent figure quoted in connection with petroleum imports is slightly high. During 1975, the U.S. imported 37 percent of its petroleum supplies versus 40 percent in 1976. For additional data regarding the impact of petroleum price increases on this country's balance position, see James Cook, "The Invisible Crisis," *Forbes*, July 15, 1976, p. 26ff. The specific dollar estimate Cook cites closely parallels those referred to by Judelson.

11. Henry A. Kissinger, "Global Consensus and Economic Development," speech prepared for delivery to the Seventh Special Session of the UN General Assembly, September 1, 1975, p. 2.

12. Ibid., p. 4.

13. Edmund G. Brown, Jr., prerecorded political program paid for by the Brown for President Committee, delivered June 25, 1976, pp. 4–5.

14. Ibid., p. 5.

15. "Arab Oil Not Critical Nobel Economists Say," *Atlanta Constitution*, November 11, 1973, p. 1A.

16. Brown, prerecorded political program, p. 5.

17. Ad Hoc Committee on Energy report, p. 1.

18. Comments by Representative Thomas Ashley, chairman of the Ad Hoc Committee on Energy, about the time required to formulate a comprehensive energy policy and underscore these points regarding the tenacity of the "energy problem." Speaking about the comprehensive program that his committee was to recommend to the House of Representatives, Ashley emphasized that, notwithstanding the "broad-gauged" quality of his committee's proposals (which had been drawn in large measure from President Carter's own energy plan), many more problem-solving efforts would be required in the future. "What Congress is going to do this year, 1977, is to build a structure on which future initiatives can be . . . added. I think by the year 1985 we'll see that the initiatives that are in place this year, plus those, that follow, will indeed cause us to achieve the goals that have been set forth . . . obviously what we're talking about

is an envolving strategy." Thomas Ashley, on the CBS "Face the Nation" broadcast, July 17, 1977.

19. Clayton Jones, "Small Dams—Enough To Power New York City," *Christian Science Monitor*, July 29, 1977, p. 1. Also see the remarks by Congress-woman Martha Keys entitled "Energy: Think Small," *Congressional Record*, August 1977, p. E5004.

20. T.W. Kielen, "Fuel from Grass, Sawdust Ignites Commercial Interest," *Christian Science Monitor*, August 16, 1977, p. 11.

Index